Beethoven

Beethoven

R.M. James

Series Editors
Michael and Mollie Hardwick

Evergreen Lives

ISBN 0 7127 0001 3

Series Editors
Michael and Mollie Hardwick

Design by Roy Lee

Production by Bob Towell

Colour Separations
by
D.S. Colour International Limited, London
Photo-typesetting
by
Sayers Clark Limited, Croydon, Surrey

Printed and bound in Spain by
TONSA, San Sebastian

Contents

Select Bibliography

DENIS ARNOLD and NIGEL FORTUNE - *The Beethoven Companion* (London 1971).

E. FORBES (Editor) - *Thayer's Life of Beethoven* (Princetown 1964).

M. HAMBURGER (Editor) - Beethoven: Letters, Journals and Conversations (London 1966).

DAVID JACOBS - Beethoven (New York 1970).

GEORGE R. MAREK - Beethoven (New York 1969).

ATES ORGA - *Beethoven, his life and times* (Tunbridge Wells 1978).

ANTON F. SCHINDLER, D. MacARDLE (Editor), C. S. JOLLY (Trans) - *Beethoven as I knew him* (London 1966).

JOSEPH SCHMIDT-GORG and HANS SCHMIDT (Editors) - *Ludwig van Beethoven: Bicentienial Edition 1770-1970* (Hamburg 1974).

P. M. YOUNG - *Beethoven* (London 1966).

Chronology

1770   Beethoven born in Bonn, 17 December.

1778   His first public performance as a pianist, 26 March.

1783   Employed as court theatre musician.

1787   Befriended by Breuning family. His first trip to Vienna. Meets Mozart. Returns to Bonn due to his mother's fatal illness.

1788   His talents recognised by Count Waldstein.

1790   Meets Haydn for the first time.

1791   Death of Mozart, 5 December.

1792   Beethoven settles in Vienna in November. He becomes Haydn's pupil. His father's death, 18 December.

1796   Tour in Northern Europe as piano virtuoso.

1799   First Symphony and *Pathétique* Sonata first performed. Meets Guilietta Guicciardi.

1801   *Moonlight* Sonata first performed.

1802   Writes the *Heiligenstadt Testament* from

despair at increasing deafness.

1803 *Kreutzer* Sonata first performed.

1805 *Eroica* Symphony first performed. First version of *Fidelio* presented. Beethoven in love with Therese and Josephine von Brunswick.

1806 First performance of Violin Concerto.

1808 Offered post of Kapellmeister at Court of Westphalia. Fifth and *Pastoral* Symphonies first performed.

1809 Given a pension by Archduke Rudolph and other patrons to remain in Vienna. Death of Haydn, 31 May. *Emperor* Concerto first performed. French occupy Vienna in October.

1812 Begins writing to 'The Immortal Beloved'.

1814 Revised version of *Fidelio* performed. Napoleon defeated and Congress of Vienna convenes.

1815 Last public appearance as a pianist, 25 January. Death of his brother Carl. Beethoven claims guardianship of his nephew Karl, leading to long litigation against Karl's mother.

1818 *Hammerklavier* Sonata.

1823 *Diabelli* Variations.

1824 First performance of *Missa Solemnis* and Ninth ('Choral') Symphony. Begins last Quartets.

1826 His ward Karl attempts suicide.

1827 Death of Beethoven, 26 March.

Introduction

THERE EXIST MANY PORTRAITS of Ludwig van
Beethoven; he was not averse to giving a sitting or
two, and artists and sculptors were finding him an
interesting subject even before he had scaled the
heights of fame. The most attractive of all portrayals
is Christian Horneman's miniature, dated 1803,
depicting him as sensitive, serious, and remarkably
neat - he had not yet lapsed into the unkemptness
which we more readily associate with him. It is
Franz Klein's bust, based on a life-mask of 1812,
which shows us perhaps more accurately than any
other representation the Beethoven whom there is
no mistaking - awesome, scowling, the tormented
revolutionary, condemned to deafness, chronic ill
health, and solitary despair.

If there are any portraits of him smiling, one has
yet to see them. Few sitters smiled in those days, and
he was a man who took himself and his art more
seriously than most, so those stern expressions may
be presumed to show him as he preferred to be
regarded. They accord with all that has been written
of his pugnacity and capacity for wrath, and that
lifelong resentment of any gesture seemingly
intended to patronize or belittle him. Indeed, by the
time Klein made his mask and model, Beethoven
had little left to amuse him; yet the image of a man
constantly at odds with the world and life, living in
isolation and squalor, is partly misleading, and
makes it worth recalling a description of him by one

who knew him better than most, his biographer, Anton Schindler:

> His build was thick-set, with big bones and strong muscles; his extra-large head was covered with long, unkempt, almost completely grey hair, giving him a somewhat savage appearance. His forehead was high and broad, his eyes small and brown, almost retreating into his head when he laughed... When he smiled, a most benevolent and amiable look spread over his face, especially encouraging to strangers with whom he spoke. His laughter, on the other hand, often burst out immoderately, distorting the intelligent and strongly marked features; the huge head seemed to swell as the face became still broader, so that the whole effect was often that of a grimacing caricature.

So Beethoven smiled - laughed, even, chatted with strangers! It does not accord with the way we are conditioned to picture him; yet his smiles are often there in his music, especially in those bewitching scherzo movements which offset so gaily the sombre grandeur preceding them and disarm us ahead of the tumultuous triumph of his finales. In his way, he was a sociable man. He was familiar in the cafés and taverns of Vienna, drinking his share and taking a full part in the talk, even if he would keep going on about art and the responsibilities of the artist. For all his eccentricities and low flashpoint, he never lacked friends.

He loved Nature and the outdoors, exulting in the beauties of the Vienna Woods, familiar enough with their bird-song to be able to reproduce its varying sounds long after he could no longer hear them. During the summer months, his sallow, liverish complexion glowed red and brown from the sunshine, like a russet apple. But, like any of his works, the mood could change abruptly, as Schindler pictures so well:

> His eyes could suddenly grow unnaturally large and prominent, rolling and flashing, their pupils usually turned upward - or quite motionless,

staring fixedly ahead when some idea seized him.
When that happened, his whole appearance would
be changed, with such an obviously inspired and
impressive look that his small figure would seem
to measure up to his mighty spirit. These moments
of sudden inspiration often came over him, even in
the jolliest company, and also in the street,
attracting the notice of passers-by. Only his
gleaming eyes and his face showed what was going
on inside him…

What was going on inside him we cannot fully
know, until we know what inspiration is and where
it comes from. What we can conjecture is that he had
'heard' something, or felt it, or just sensed it, and
that his natural receptiveness had alerted him to take
note of and hold on to it, to carry it back to those
littered rooms where he lived, untidy and alone,
there eventually to make use of it with the sublime
creativeness of which only he was capable.
Wherever he was, and whatever he was doing,
Beethoven remained ever alert to the incoming
messages. His art was his life, a life of slow,
painstaking toil and monotony, attended by anxiety
and despair, from which taking country walks,
laughing with friends and chatting to strangers were
merely diversions.

At the day's end there was no escaping into
calming domesticity. He had a number of love
affairs, but almost all the women concerned were
beyond his reach, aristocratic and destined to
marry within their own class, or married already. It
has been suggested that he preferred it to be like
that, so that he could savour frustration and at the
same time keep his independence to live in his
Bohemian way. Whoever his 'Immortal Beloved'
was, that theory goes, he might not have bared his
emotions to her so readily if she had been likely to
take him up on them. He would have been
disastrous as a husband, as he would a parent: his
bungling though sincere efforts to bring up his
nephew Karl, away from the influence of the
immoral mother whom the boy loved, are evidence
of that. No doubt the aristocratic young ladies who

flirted with Beethoven did so partly for amusement, and because it was daring to sport with a half-tame savage, but always knowing that safe lines of retreat were open to them, and that, for all his defiance of social conventions, there were boundaries which even he could not cross.

So always, in the last resort, he was driven back into himself; and Ludwig van Beethoven's inner solitude was far intenser, more agonizing than it is given to most men to endure. From the earliest days of his fame he had been growing aware that deafness was overtaking him. It cost him his career as the most brilliant pianist of his age; it drove him to consider taking his own life; it reduced him to a cripple who could only converse with others by getting them to write down what they wanted to say to him, and who could not even hear the music he went on composing, which, paradoxically, became greater and greater, and more and more innovative and inventive, the deafer he grew.

In fact, that is not so paradoxical at all: a composer is less dependent on the acuteness of his hearing than the layman supposes. Because some of Beethoven's works contain almost unplayable or unsingable passages does not imply that his judgment was impaired because he was deaf. They were simply beyond the capacities of the musicians of his time, of which he was so far in advance. Their successors have learnt to play and sing them, thereby extending the range of musical technique. He knew precisely what effects he was demanding, because he could hear them accomplished in his mind.

Perhaps it is not going too far to suggest that Beethoven's deafness intensified his art, sparing him the distractions of everyday noise. He had heard all he needed to hear in his youth, had noted the possibilities of the human voice and all the combinations of instruments, had captured for ever the uplifting sounds of Nature by which his inspiration never ceased to be stimulated. He held all these in his mind, idealized and safe where they could never be overlaid and spoiled.

That is not to say that he valued being deaf. It caused him great misery and exacerbated his less agreeable tendencies. He had always been aware of his worth, refusing to kow-tow to any man or woman, of whatever rank or riches. The tradesmen's-entrance servility of Haydn and Mozart towards their patrons was never for Beethoven: he strode in by the front door and made for the top table, offended if he did not find his place next to his employer. Inevitably, he was often snubbed or rebuked, whereupon he spoke his mind with vehemence enough to make strong men blench and ladies succumb to the vapours. It gave rise to much mirth among the bystanders, some of whom would have been positively disappointed not to have witnessed one of the celebrated eruptions.

What they did not always see was the aftermath. When his rage had abated, Beethoven, who would bend the knee to none if expected to, would sincerely beg pardon for his offensiveness. Like the sunshine which follows the thunderstorm in his *Pastoral* Symphony, his smile and apologies would make amends for everything. He knew he behaved disgracefully. When he railed, it was less against individuals than against life itself, which he felt had hung so many injustices and handicaps about his burly but sensitive shoulders. He had been quite dandified as a young man, but became so habitually dishevelled later that one is tempted to suspect that he cultivated it, along with his grubbiness, his spitting, his disordered lifestyle, as the outward reminder of that resolution of his youth: 'I will take Fate by the throat!'

But his alternately raging and melancholic personality was far from wholly self-centred. His deepest concern was for art, and, inextricable from it, for mankind at large. He did not deliberately employ music as a means of propaganda for freedom's cause; yet the kind of music he instinctively wrote, and the type of man he was, and the state of ferment existing in Europe at the time he lived, all boiled up together to make a heady beverage capable of nourishing fighters for freedom everywhere and throughout all subsequent ages. His shout for democracy was abstract and tuneful, but its message was none the less potent for that.

Ludwig van Beethoven

> Liberty and progress are the goals of art, just as of
> life in general... Words are bound in chains, but
> happily sounds are still free.

It is wholly appropriate, musically and emotionally,
that the exultant *Ode to Joy* from his masterwork,
the Ninth Symphony, should have been chosen as
the official anthem of that latter-day brotherhood of
free nations, the Council of Europe; while it is fully
justified that Beethoven should so often, and in so
wide a range of contexts, have been declared
'music's Shakespeare'.

Michael and Mollie Hardwick

Seeds of Genius

1770 – 1784

BEETHOVEN'S LIFE STORY begins with an uncert-
ainty: no one can say exactly when in December
1770 he was born.

The first known reference to him, in the parish
records of St Remigius Church, Bonn, in West
Germany, states that on 17 December 1770 there
took place the baptism of Ludwig, son of Johann
and Maria Magdalena van Beethoven. Because of
the high rate of infant mortality in those times it was
customary to have children baptized as soon as
possible after birth, so it is likely that he had been
born that same day, or at the earliest the day before.
At any rate, the 17th has become accepted as the
date on which one of the greatest creative geniuses
the world has known first saw light.

He was Johann and Maria Magdalena's second
son, a previous one having died a week after birth.
Of a total of seven children only three survived, all
boys: Ludwig, Carl and Johann. Ludwig was born
at 515 Bongasse, now No. 20, the Beethovenhaus, a
light and spacious museum to his memory. In 1770
it was quite different. The Beethoven family
occupied only the attic flat at the back of the
building; the rest of the house was occupied by
musicians of the court orchestra, colleagues of
Beethoven's father. The room in which he was born
measured about two metres square and had one tiny
window, overlooking a stable yard. Nowadays it
looks on to beautifully planned and kept gardens.

The family was Flemish in origin, as the prefix 'van' denotes, with ancestors who were artisans and tradespeople. It was Beethoven's grandfather, also a Ludwig though keeping the Flemish spelling, Lodewijk, who began the association with professional musicianship. A talented violinist and bass singer, he had started his career as a cathedral chorister. At eighteen he moved to Louvain in Belgium, where he became conductor of the choir of St Peter's Church, and later *Musicus*, director, to the local Court. In 1732 he moved to Bonn to join the court orchestra of the Elector and Archbishop of Cologne, Maximilian Friedrich. It was his final move. In the forty years he lived at Bonn he rose through the court ranks, becoming *Kapellmeister*, choir director, in 1761.

He was an amiable man, whose appearance and manner to some extent prefigured his tempestuous grandson. He had a determined personality and was described by a contemporary as 'short of stature, muscular, with extremely animated eyes, and greatly respected as a musician', all features of Beethoven himself in later life. The only shadow over Lodewijk's contentment was that his wife Maria Josepha became an alcoholic and in her later years had to be taken into care. Excessive drinking was a characteristic which her son Johann was to develop.

The Bonn of Beethoven's grandfather was a prosperous city governed by the benign Elector-Archbishop Prince Clemens August, a well-known patron of the arts. Bonn had been largely destroyed in the wars and upheavals of the last years of the seventeenth century, and the Electors Joseph Clemens and Clemens August had employed the leading architects to plan its reconstruction and design palaces for them in keeping with their status as secular and ecclesiastical princes. Although the breaking up of Germany into small, self-governing states and principalities did nothing for political or social progress, the inter-state rivalry to which it gave rise stimulated artistic life. To have a grander palace and a more renowned orchestra than those of surrounding courts was the aim of most of their rulers: the Duke of Weimar once put his prized

Johann Sebastian Bach under arrest for seeking permission to leave his service. With the proximity of refined and elegant eighteenth century France influencing the Rhineland states, and electors determined to show off their magnificence through the arts, the Beethovens were able to enjoy two-and-a-half relatively prosperous generations in Bonn.

As a member of the court orchestra, Lodewijk was able to find a place in it for his son, and from the age of twelve Johann played the violin under his father's direction. Life at Court was lavish: Elector Clemens August enjoyed ceremony and elaborate operatic and ballet performances, especially ones prominently featuring pretty girls. Although a court musician's salary was enough for modest living, Lodewijk ran a wine shop as a sideline to supplement his income. Unfortunately his best, though unpaying, customer was his wife. Their son Johann had a sombre, introspective nature, and this together with the demands of orchestral playing drove him increasingly to follow his mother's example and seek comfort in the bottle. His fits of depression and consequent drunkenness, followed by debilitating hangovers, became so frequent that he was forced eventually to leave the orchestra for the much less significant job of a tenor singer in the Elector's chapel.

In 1767 Johann van Beethoven married Maria Magdalena Keverich, then aged twenty-one and already a widow. Lodewijk had fiercely opposed the match from the beginning. Maria Magdelena was the daughter of a cook, her first husband had been a chamberlain in the electoral household, and she herself was a maid-servant. Lodewijk saw her as interested in his son's money. There could scarcely have been much fortune for her to hunt, though as the son of a well-placed musician Johann's social standing was higher than hers. She was a slightly-built, pretty girl of a patient disposition, which she must have needed in view of his alternating sullen and drunken moods. Beethoven never lost a deep fondness for his mother and remained closely attached to her until her death when he was sixteen.

Lodewijk died in Bonn when his grandson Ludwig was three years old, in 1773. The following year the Beethovens, unable to keep up the rental of 515 Bongasse, moved to a house in the Rheingasse (now No. 7) belonging to a family named Fischer, who continued to live in part of it and found their tenants 'righteous and peaceful' under Maria Magdalena's rule. Johann still occupied a respectable place on the periphery of the Court, mixing with minor officials and receiving a regular salary, which he supplemented by taking private music pupils. Gradually, however, he began to imbibe more heavily; his teaching dwindled in turn. Had Maria Magdalena been of a more forceful nature she might have been able to take control of the situation, but she was never a robustly healthy woman and could only watch her husband deteriorating, while she did what she could to mend and patch the family's clothes and eke out what money was available for paying bills. The Fischers were struck by her serious expression and noticed that she never laughed at anything. She had little enough to laugh about, and it may be that the tuberculosis from which she would die in 1787 was already beginning to show. She, too, went gradually into decline. At school Ludwig was noted to be dirty and apparently neglected. Formal schooling, however, was to be the least part of his education, for by the time he was five he was learning the piano and violin, in a determined if unorthodox fashion.

Johann's perception had not been so dulled that he could not recognize exceptional musical talent in his son. It was something which all German and Austrian parents looked for in their children in those days, when the example of the child prodigy Wolfgang Amadeus Mozart, born 1756, was there for all to pray their offspring might emulate. Also the son of a court musician, Mozart had toured the courts and capitals of Europe some fifteen years before this time. He had played to Marie Antoinette at the French Court and before the Emperor of Austria. His talents astounded all who heard him. At the keyboard he could rival any adult professional; as a composer he had published sonatas before he was ten. On a visit to the Vatican he had astonished everyone by returning to his lodgings after hearing a single performance of a mass for choir and soloists and writing the piece out perfectly from memory.

As a result of these feats, unquestioned fame and promise of wealth - though more promise than actuality, it transpired - had come to the Mozart family, and Johann van Beethoven, aware that his son was also the possessor of great natural gifts which might lead to that same desired end, was determined to mould his own infant prodigy. Unfortunately, circumstances were somewhat different. For one thing the temperaments of the two boys were dissimilar. Young Mozart had delighted in his success and travelling constantly, in company with his gifted sister, whereas Beethoven was already showing the desire for solitude which would increase with the years. The two fathers could hardly have been different, either. Leopold Mozart was a sober man who took his role as his young son's respected manager seriously, while Johann's irresponsibility was increasing. Although Beethoven could in all probability have fulfilled his side of the creation of a new prodigy, his father found the demands on him too great. After one attempt in March 1778 to launch his son the idea seems to have been dropped.

The boy's training, however, was not discontinued. A cousin of his mother's, Franz Rovantini, also a court orchestral player and fellow lodger in the house, taught him violin and viola. Then from 1779 another resident, Tobias Pfeiffer, gave him piano lessons. These were professional musicians, and though their methods may have been curious, even cruel at times - as when Pfeiffer, returning with Johann late at night and drunk, dragged young Ludwig from bed to give him a lesson - their standards were high, and their pupil was able to learn much from them.

Much of his ability sprang from within himself, though. Like Mozart before him, he was composing from an early age. How much was his own and how much owed to the guidance of his father or teachers cannot be known, but his first published set of three piano sonatas was claimed to have been started at the age of four. When the sonatas were published he was thirteen, though reputedly eleven. The dedication today appears cloyingly sycophantic, but this was the age when aristocratic patronage was at its height, and such niceties needed to be observed to keep masters' tempers sweet. At about this time Mozart's patron, the Archbishop of Salzburg, had him literally kicked down his palace stairs, and Haydn had only recently ceased having to eat his meals in the servants' hall. To the Elector Maximilian Friedrich in 1783 Ludwig (though certainly the wording was Johann's) wrote:

> Serene Highness, When I was four, music became my first youthful occupation. Made familiar so early in life with a Muse which made my head echo with pure harmonies, she became a dear friend to me and I felt that in return I also became dear to her. Now I have already reached my eleventh year; but since those early days, whenever I felt inspired, I could hear the Muse whisper - try to write down those harmonies in your head. But I am only eleven years old, I thought. How can I possibly appear as a composer...

Ludwig, who had only elementary schooling, learning a little Italian and some Latin and finding mathematics difficult, never fitted in entirely among his schoolmates. They nicknamed him 'the Spaniard' because of his dark complexion. Other descriptions of him as a boy emphasize the stocky appearance, the square jaw, the massive head with its curls and those other features which have become so well known from the later portraits. He spent a lot of his time alone, and even as a boy preferred his own company in long walks by the Rhine to playing games with schoolfellows. Domestic and musical pressures were perhaps partly the cause of all this. Wisely, on completion of the elementary stage of schooling, Johann took him away from the classroom, and from then on his time was devoted entirely to music.

In his attempt to equip him as an all-round musician, and perhaps bearing in mind from his own experience that a fall from the court orchestra could be cushioned by a landing in the Elector's chapel, Johann set him to learn the organ, initially under the old court organist Aegidius van den Eeden and then under his successor, Christian Gottlob Neefe. Beethoven took to the organ readily, calling it later 'the sovereign of all instruments'. But more important than his introduction to it was his meeting with Neefe.

Neefe had arrived in Bonn in 1779 and two years later was appointed court organist, despite vigorous protests at the post being given to a North German Calvinist. A man of wide interests, a composer and writer of musical criticism, he recognized Beethoven's genius at once, and began to broaden and civilize his studies, adding composition and the reading of good literature and philosophy to organ lessons. Neefe was among the band of men who were beginning to struggle against the restraint of court employment at the end of the eighteenth century. Even the greatest geniuses up to this time had all relied on Court or Church for their subsistence. The entire Bach family had to bear this servitude grudgingly; Mozart and Haydn only partially freed themselves from it towards the end of their lives, and in Mozart's case it proved to be a ruinous step, resulting in his death in abject poverty and burial in an unmarked pauper's grave in Vienna. In keeping with the spirit of the times emanating from France, and inspired by Rousseau's writings in particular, Neefe saw the creative artist as more than the lackey of a patron whose tastes might be inferior and whose demands might be restricting to the impulses of real talent or genius. This spirit, among much else, he infused into the young Beethoven. It was to be a vital notion, catching hold and sticking in his mind and leading him to become the first composer of any note to hold out for artistic freedom and the right to write as he chose, not as a patron directed. This giant step forward, to the benefit of all successive composers, came directly from the influence of Neefe, though in Beethoven's personality the seed he cast found exceptionally fertile soil in which to propagate.

Neefe introduced him to the classical authors as well as to contemporary German writings such as those of Lessing and Schiller. In music, Neefe set great store by the works of the Bach family, at that time not widely or properly appreciated. He brought J.S. Bach's *Well-tempered Clavier*, the 48 preludes and fugues in all major and minor keys, to Beethoven's notice. These works, many intensely difficult and often referred to as constituting the pianist's 'Old Testament' (with Beethoven's 26 sonatas dubbed the 'New Testament'), were a joy to the ten-year-old Ludwig, and he gave intense study to them. On the other hand Neefe began to suggest that a greater degree of flexibility of form and freedom of expression might be necessary to convey ideas which the existing, highly formalized styles might inhibit. Though this was only the first hint at the 'Romantic' style which was to engage Beethoven later, the notion was implanted early.

So impressive was young Beethoven's progress under Neefe that he was able to deputize entirely for him in the organist's absence, and before he was twelve he was able to take over chapel services. When in 1783 Neefe took over the court theatre he installed Beethoven as chembalist, or harpsichord accompanist to the theatre orchestra. This involved attending all rehearsals and playing for performances. It shows what degree of talent and maturity the thirteen-year-old possessed, and marks the beginning of official recognition of him. When the new Elector Maximilian Franz succeeded to the archbishopric in 1784, Beethoven was already established as unpaid official assistant court organist. He was now a professional musician, which must have compensated Johann to some extent for having missed out with him as child prodigy.

What must have impressed Ludwig and his family more, however, was the glowing, if self-advertising, testimonial Neefe had published in the Bonn periodical, Cramer's *Magazin der Musik*, on 2 March 1783:

Louis van Beethoven...a boy of eleven years old and of a most promising talent...plays the clavier very skilfully and with power, reads at sight very well and - in a nutshell - plays chiefly the *Well Tempered Clavier* of Sebastian Bach, which Herr Neefe put in his hands. Whoever knows this collection of preludes and fugues in all the keys - which might almost be called the *ne plus ultra* of our art - will know what this means. He is now training him in composition and for his encouragement has had nine variations for the pianoforte, written by him on a march, engraved at Mannheim. This young genius deserves to be given financial help so that he may travel and will undoubtedly become a second Wolfgang Amadeus Mozart if he continues as he has begun.

Beethoven never forgot the kindness of Neefe in this and in much else. Ten years later at the time of his departure for Vienna he was moved to write to him: 'I thank you for the advice you have so often given me about my progress in my divine art. If I ever become a great man, you too will share in my success.'

'Your True Friend Waldstein'

1784 – 1792

BEETHOVEN'S EARLY CAREER as a professional musician coincided happily with the installation in 1784 of the Elector Maximilian Franz. This affable, twenty-eight-year-old son of the Empress Maria Theresa and brother of the Emperor Joseph II of Austria was an enlightened and liberal man, anxious to encourage the arts and sciences in his principality. Concerned with standards of education in general, he raised the *Hochschule* in Bonn to the status of university, and set about enhancing the city's reputation as a musical centre. Neefe was able to report in the *Magazin der Musik*:

> Our city is becoming more and more attractive to music-lovers through the gracious patronage of our beloved Elector. He has a large collection of the most beautiful music and is expending a great deal every day to augment it. It is to him, too, that we owe the privilege of often hearing good virtuosi on various instruments...The love of music is increasing greatly among the inhabitants.

It was magnanimous - or perhaps hopeful - of Neefe to write thus. As a result of a survey of musical resources, carried out at the Elector's command, Neefe had suffered a cut in annual salary to 200 florins, while the hitherto unpaid Beethoven had been granted 150, with a pat on the head: 'He has good ability, is still young and his conduct is quiet and upright.'

29

The same could not be said of his father, however. His voice was noted to be 'definitely decaying'. Long service, 'respectable conduct', and poor circumstances were urged in mitigation, and he was kept on.

Not content to maintain an orchestra in Bonn, Maximilian assembled one to go with him on visits to his second baroque castle at Brühl. Beethoven was among their number. He supplemented his stipend by giving piano lessons, bringing some financial relief to his increasingly suffering family. Although he hated the time-consuming demands of teaching, it provided an even more valuable benefit than money: it brought him into contact with upper-middle class families and eventually the aristocracy.

A friend of his, Franz Wegeler, a hard-up medical student (later to be one of Beethoven's physicians) had been befriended by the wealthy and highly cultivated von Breuning family of Bonn. Their daughter Eleonore needed piano lessons and Wegeler intro-duced Beethoven, recollecting in later life how 'Beethoven's first joyous emotions found vent here. He was soon treated as one of the children, spending not only the greater part of his days in the house, but also many nights. He felt that he was free here, he moved about without constraint, everything conspired to make him cheerful and develop his mind.'

It has also been suggested that he conceived some-thing of an infatuation for Eleonore; but it was Wegeler whom she married in 1802.

It was in this enlightened household that Beethoven made his first acquaintance with German literature, especially poetry, which was to become of such im-portance to him. He also began to acquire some social graces. Coming from his underprivileged background he had much to learn of the formal graces of the eighteenth-century salon. He acquired them, but never made himself their slavish servant. Even at this stage he would kow-tow to no one, saying what he felt and not fearing to rebuff anyone he suspected of looking down on him. Some people dismissed him as boorish, but others were amused, and many of the acquaintances he made at this time became friends for life.

He was encouraged to enrol at the University, where he studied literature and philosophy, becoming especially familiar with the works of Shakespeare and Kant. A love of Shakespeare, whose ideas of the dignity of mankind, the value of freedom and the virtues of love and friendship Beethoven was to share and express so fervently, never left him. He also benefited from the extra-curricular aspects of university life, enjoying the company of professors, fellow students and leading figures of literature and the arts in their favourite eating places.

The Elector Maximilian's interest in him continued, meanwhile; and in April 1787 he carried in his pocket an introduction from Maximilian to his brother, the Emperor of Austria, when he visited Vienna for the first time, at the age of sixteen.

Vienna was, quite simply, the musical capital of the world. In 1787 music was everywhere. The aristocracy, drawn there by the allure of the liberal court of Emperor Joseph II, held its own salons in the drawing-rooms of the many great town houses. Opera played every night in the theatres; Joseph himself had inaugurated the new Burgtheater. Like his mother, the Emperor was a fine musician and their enthusiasm percolated down through Viennese society to the level of street cafés in which music was always to be heard; in later years Schubert and Brahms were both to augment their incomes by playing in cafés in Vienna.

Beethoven's initial reaction to Vienna could have been predicted: he was thrilled. Vienna's likely reaction to him was less certain. As he did throughout his life, he stood out as a 'provincial', with his pronounced soft-spoken Rhineland accent. His clothes were unfashionable, and owed nothing to good taste. He was defensively aggressive, demanding the attention due to his self-valuation. He made it plain that he had not come there to perform background salon music; he had come to be listened to with respect.

Whatever impressions may have been gained superficially from his speech and appearance were soon swept aside when he did perform. The force and vigour of his piano playing even then impressed his hearers and gave hints of what was to come. Although he met the Emperor briefly it was not the high moment of his visit: that came when he met Mozart.

Mozart was then thirty and at the height of his powers and popularity. As one of the two greatest composers alive - the other being the much older Haydn - Mozart was accustomed to being expected to listen to aspiring musicians visiting Vienna, and it was with some indifference that he received the young Beethoven. On hearing the young man play a piece which Mozart assumed to be a much-practised set-piece he was duly unimpressed. Typically, the impetuous Beethoven requested a theme from Mozart on which he would extemporize, there and then. Mozart provided it, and listened with growing interest as the young pianist enlarged on the theme, varied it, and wrought it about with such inventiveness and power that Mozart was forced to say to a companion, 'Keep your eyes on him; some day he will give the world something to talk about.'

As a result of this audition Beethoven engaged himself for lessons from Mozart. Unfortunately, the remarkable association which might have resulted was never to come about, for within a fortnight Beethoven was hurrying home to be with his dying mother.

Although his father's letter had urged him to come home, he had not conveyed the gravity of the situation. Beethoven found his mother in the last stages of consumption. She lingered till July, the family having to watch helplessly her slow and painful deterioration. Beethoven was deeply upset at her death. She had been the unifying factor in their family, and in spite of her husband's conduct had always urged the children to understand and respect him. Beethoven wrote to the friend in Augsburg from whom he had had to borrow the money for his sudden return journey, 'She was such a dear, kind mother to me, my best friend. Oh! who was happier than I, when I could still utter the sweet name of mother and it was heard and answered?'

To add to his troubles, he found that his father had lapsed into almost continual drunkenness, and the family's affairs were in total disarray, Johann having sold or pawned many of their possessions to

buy drink. With the ability for quick and decisive
action when it was needed which would reveal itself
later in his life, Ludwig decided to take charge. To
begin with he returned to his post in the court
orchestra, which would bring in some money at
least. A housekeeper was employed to look after his
two younger brothers and the sole surviving sister,
who would soon enough die, aged eighteen months.
In a final move, Ludwig went to law in 1789 and got
Johann deprived of his authority as head of the
family, taking the reponsibility on himself. That
same year Johann was retired on half pay. To spare
his father's feelings, Ludwig allowed him to draw
the salary in person and then pass it on to him for the
benefit of the family. The scene must have been a
sad and shameful one for all involved, but it had to
be gone through each time; the boys regularly had to
scour the taverns of the city to find their father, or
retrieve him from the police.

A newcomer to Maximilian's Court in 1788 was
Count Ferdinand Waldstein, one of the young
Elector's closest friends. He was a leading light in
Bonn society and had connections in high places in
Vienna. As a talented musician and composer, he
could not fail to perceive the budding genius of
Ludwig van Beethoven, nine years his junior, and he
determined to help him in any way he could, giving
him a piano worthy of his accomplished and notice-
ably original mode of playing. 'His technique,' wrote
one who watched him not long after this time, 'is so
different from the traditional technique of piano-
playing, as if he had wanted to develop a completely
individual approach towards his present achievement.' Waldstein also gave him money, which had to
be disguised as gratuities from the Elector, so as not to
offend the prickly young man.

The Elector had decided to found a National
Theatre, and Beethoven was employed in its orchestra, first as a viola player and then harpsichord
accompanist. It gave him excellent new experience,
while keeping on his post as organist, adding theatre
and ballet music to his range. He was also working at
composition. A melancholy chance to get himself
known was provided by the death of the Elector's

33

brother, Joseph II, in 1790. Beethoven was commissioned by the Artists' Association in Bonn to produce a cantata to mark the occurrence. He completed the work for chorus and orchestra in three weeks, and by the standards of the times was thought to have produced a piece of remarkable difficulty. In spite of pleas from the Musical Association to make it less taxing on singers and orchestra he refused to change a note. Difficult though the work may have been (it has been suggested that there are traces in the third part, 'Then men shall rise up to the light', of the setting he was to use for Schiller's lines in the Finale of his Ninth Symphony thirty years later) the Society must have been impressed by it, for they required another cantata from him six months later to mark the accession as Emperor of Leopold II, Joseph's younger brother. These two cantatas in themselves represent no specifically great achievement, but through the intercession of Count Waldstein they came to the notice of the most revered composer then alive, Joseph Haydn: Mozart had died at the end of 1791, aged thirty-six.

Haydn, at sixty, had to his name a huge body of work - over one hundred symphonies, operas, oratorios, sonatas, quartets; virtually every form of composition had been touched on in his long career, all managed with the grace and facility which established his fame. Not only was he recognized in his homeland of Austria, but in Britain, where he made tours to great acclaim. His reception in London had been overwhelming and resulted in many commissions, and Oxford University made him a Doctor of Music. It was while passing through Bonn on his return from one of these visits to England that Haydn was prevailed on by Waldstein to hear the *Cantata on the Death of Joseph II*. 'Papa' Haydn was immensely impressed - enough to encourage the Elector Maximilian to send the young composer to Vienna, though nothing came of the proposal. Passing through Bonn again in the summer of 1792, Haydn once more made a point of listening to Beethoven's playing and compositions. In the intervening two years Beethoven had been composing songs, mainly to texts by Goethe, and had by then produced over fifty piano pieces, among them the Thirteen Variations. This time Haydn was not prepared to stop at a mere recommendation; he was determined to have the emerging genius as his pupil. Waldstein discussed the matter with the Elector, who granted Beethoven a subsistence allowance on top of his continuing salary, now more than doubled to 400 Fl. In addition to this the Count made funds available for him to travel and to equip himself in a style appropriate to the fashionable Hapsburg capital.

Careful as ever, Beethoven made arrangements for his family's well-being after his departure by ensuring that the pension and part of his own salary would go to the education of his two brothers, then aged sixteen and eighteen, Carl studying music and Johann pharmacy.

Before leaving Bonn at the beginning of November 1792, Beethoven was presented with an album by his friends. In it they had written snatches of verse and notes of farewell. 'Lorchen' von Breuning quoted the poet Herder: 'May friendship and goodness grow like the evening shadow until the sun of life sets.' Count Waldstein, surely a patron to rank with any in history, wrote:

> Dear Beethoven: At last you are going to Vienna in the fulfilment of a wish that you have long cherished in vain. The genius of music weeps and mourns the death of its disciple, Mozart. It has found a refuge in the inexhaustible Haydn, but no permanent home, and now it longs to unite with a higher spirit. May you, through your unceasing hard work, receive Mozart's spirit from the hands of Haydn.

Leaving Bonn on the foggy morning of 2 November Beethoven was not to know that he would never return there. With the death of his father on 18 December of that year, and the flight of his brothers from the invading French three years later, all connection with his birthplace, save in his affectionate memories, was severed.

Early Years in Vienna

1792 – 1799

THE JOURNEY TO VIENNA was not an easy one. The armies of Revolutionary France were already threatening the Rhinelands and Beethoven had to bribe his coachman to pass through the Prussian army, which, under General Hesse, was rushing to support the taxed and slender forces of the Rhineland states. But he arrived at last on the evening of 10 November and wasted no time in making contacts and setting himself up in the city. Beethoven was never to settle in one house in Vienna: in the thirty-five years he lived there he occupied some thirty houses or apartments, frequently moving to rooms he found cheaper, or quieter, or where he could play the piano as loudly as he wished, or where it was easier to receive pupils; or, simply, because his restless nature demanded a change. His first lodging was an attic room, exchanged within weeks for the house of Prince Karl Lichnowsky. The change did not signify advancement, however; it was quite common for the Viennese nobility to rent out unused rooms.

Realizing that if he was to make a mark musically it would have to be as a performer above all, Beethoven's first necessity was to equip himself for the salon life of the Viennese aristocracy to whom he needed to demonstrate his capabilities. Out of Waldstein's benefaction he bought a piano, of course, but also new and more fashionable clothes, silk stockings and knee breeches, velvet coats, good shirts and cravats, and he even began to take dancing lessons. He also made early contact with Haydn.

The relationship between Beethoven and Haydn did not prove an easy or truly successful one, however. Haydn, highly respected and much sought after both in Vienna and abroad, had perhaps underestimated the difficulties involved in teaching formal academic musical theory, counterpoint and techniques of composition to a young man full of new, powerful and, to his more sedate elder, revolutionary ideas. Beethoven admired Haydn and dutifully completed the work he was set, but soon became discouraged when much of that work remained uncorrected, and what was looked over drew adverse comment. Of the two hundred or so examples extant, only forty show signs of having been examined by Haydn. Beethoven's grasp of counterpoint and general theory was weak, which must have irritated his distinguished teacher, who would expect to take such grounding for granted. Also, the two were quite different in background and temperament.

Haydn started life in the famous boys' choir of the Viennese Royal Court, then had gone on to spend more than thirty years in the service of the Esterhazy family. He had come late in life to personal recognition and fame and the consequent financial independence which allowed him to work purely for himself. Much in demand, he still produced assiduously, but he now was free to travel and did so with enjoyment. Teaching pupils, no matter how gifted, could not rival bowing to the acclaim of audiences in London and other places where his reputation had reached. At heart, too, Haydn was a musician in the old tradition, the genius who was yet still prepared to fill the rôle of journeyman and turn out whatever a patron required of him. Beethoven, much more the man of his age and aware of the new liberalism which was sweeping Europe from France, was not prepared to put his natural genius under anyone else's orders. As the very first of his commissions in Bonn showed, his view, like Pilate's, was 'What I have written, I have written.' What he wrote often seemed to the staid Haydn unorthodox at best and at worst bizarre.

There was never a quarrel between the two men. In fact Haydn sent a glowing report to the Elector Maximilian, and even a fairly brusque direction that Beethoven needed a bigger allowance, as he personally had had to advance him some 500 florins. The simple fact was that Beethoven and Haydn were travelling along different roads. Haydn had taken the string quartet and the symphony and had made of them almost new media. He had been termed 'the father of the symphony', and he had brought *his* type of symphony to perfection. Now it was the turn of Beethoven, with his romantic and dramatic powers, to begin his reshaping of what Haydn had left him. Beethoven never lost the greatest respect for Haydn, and even delayed the publication of his first set of six String Quartets, Op.18, until they were sufficiently polished and perfected in his view to make them worthy of their dedication to Haydn.

Aware though he was of his inherent powers, he nonetheless knew that his compositional technique needed the aid of an accomplished master. Though it is for the vigour and robustness, as well as the emotional, spiritual and dramatic powers of his music that we chiefly think of Beethoven today, at this time in his life his main aim was to acquire the veneer of facility and grace which was then so much prized in Vienna. He consulted other teachers without telling Haydn, so as not to give offence. Among them was Johann Albrechtsberger, the leading compositional theorist of the day and court organist and *Kapellmeister* of St Stephen's Cathedral. Beethoven took lessons, chiefly in counterpoint, the musical art of interweaving melodies and preserving the melodic and harmonic flow simultaneously, but also in general composition. He also studied with the famous Antonio Salieri, *Kapellmeister* and composer at the Austrian Imperial Court. Beethoven's lessons with Salieri were chiefly concerned with setting fashionable texts in Italian to music for various combinations of voices. This was the age of the *soirée musicale*, and royalties from the sale of songs, for which there was a continual demand, could bring in a significant income for a young composer, especially useful to one still living on a grant from his past employer. From the period of Beethoven's study under Salieri there are almost thirty vocal trios, duets and quartet settings of one Italian poet, Metastasio, alone. But the income from song-writing was unpredictable; Beethoven knew that his name and reputation were to be made in the ballrooms and concert halls of the city. As well as studying composition he had been practising hard at his piano technique.

At the time of his arrival in Vienna the chief pianists of the city, Hummel, Wölfl and the Abbé Joseph Gelinek, specialised in technical brilliance of a stunning kind; keyboard pyrotechnics were the order of the day. Although the newer piano-forte (invented around 1710 in Italy by Christo-fouri) had supplanted the harpsichord, the techniques which the harpsichord had been best suited to display were still the most prized. Without the ability to sustain a note, its sound was produced by plectra plucking the strings, and then dying quick-ly. The piano's sound, produced by hammers hitting the strings, could be increased or reduced according to how hard the key was struck by the player, and sustained for a longer time after im-pact. The harpsichord player specialised in rapid runs and scales and in brilliantly executed musical ornamentation. The great pianists of Beethoven's youth had all been harpsichord players first and foremost, but Beethoven, ever the man of the future, had long realized the greater expressive range and tone of the piano, and it might be said that he was the first real piano virtuoso of Vienna as opposed to the greatest keyboard performer.

To establish his name Beethoven undertook open competitions with his rivals. The Abbé Gelinek, conceding victory to him, was so impress-ed by the talent of this newcomer that he intro-duced him to influential connections in the city. It did not prevent his harbouring lifelong jealousy of him, dismissing his compositions as trivia and spreading malicious tales of his revolutionary utterances. But even more than his rendering of known works, Beethoven's improvisations, the creation of music spontaneously at the keyboard, left his hearers bewildered at his powers of invention, concentration and development. This ability, which had drawn such praise from Mozart, caused J.B. Cramer, Beethoven's one-time rival who settled successfully to a musical career in London, to write in later years, 'No man in these days has heard extempore playing, unless he has heard Beethoven.'

Within three years of arriving in Vienna Beethoven had established himself at the centre of musical life; but he would never be content as a mere performer, no matter how sought after as a virtuoso or how admired as a keyboard improviser. His mind was set on the more serious matter of composition. By 1795 he had already brought out the three Trios for Piano, Violin and Cello, his Op.1, and many other chamber works. The fact that the Trios date from his Bonn period but are given the opus number One shows that Beethoven regarded his move to Vienna as the real beginning of his career. Sonatas for piano - one of which, in C, was dedicated to Eleonore von Breuning - for piano and violin, and piano and cello, all appeared at this time, as did sets of variations on popular themes including a set on 'Se vuol ballare' from Mozart's *Marriage of Figaro*. More significantly the first sketches were started for his larger orchestral works. The first two Piano Concertos, Op.15 and 19, were probably written chiefly as vehicles to display his pianistic brilliance; but the writing of a symphony showed the serious intention of Beethoven the composer asserting himself over Beethoven the performer.

Before settling to what he then imagined to be a full career as pianist and composer in the Empire's capital, Beethoven decided to undertake a series of concert tours which were to take him to Prague, Dresden, Berlin, Leipzig and Budapest. It was designed not only to be a source of money, but a way also of spreading his fame and showing off his own compositions to a new public. Although Vienna was the musical as well as the administrative capital, the other cities he visited had long traditions of musical appreciation, musical societies and music journals, and they had all heard Mozart play not many years before.

The newcomer did not suffer by comparision. The critic of the Leipzig *Allgemeine Musikalische Zeitung* wrote of him: 'Since the death of Mozart, who in this respect is for me still the *ne plus ultra*, I have never enjoyed the kind of pleasure to the degree in which it is provided by Beethoven.' By mixing his own works amongst those of the recognized masters, in a programme which displayed him as the executant of, say, Mozart or Haydn, he ensured a hearing for his compositions. He was always willing, too, to extemporize as an encore, or to undertake a challenge to compete against a local rival.

The novel and in many ways revolutionary playing of Beethoven with its sudden powerful contrasts and huge range of dynamics was considered strange in some of the cities in which he performed. In Prague he was said by a critic to have 'conquered our ears but not our hearts', though in others some members of his audiences were moved to tears by the brilliance and lyrical qualities of his playing. Audiences there were customarily restrained when it came to applauding, and he was puzzled and rather disappointed by their failure to match the Viennese rapture to which he was growing used.

In Berlin the style of reception was more as he had expected. The King of Prussia, Frederick-William II, successor of Frederick the Great, was devoted to music and was famed as having one of the finest orchestras in Europe in his employ. After hearing a concert at which Beethoven not only played some of his own works, but also improvised a series of variations on an anthem in Frederick-William's honour which had just been performed by a choir, he gave Beethoven a private audience and presented him with a gold snuff-box full of gold coins. It was a gift Beethoven always kept and of which he was inordinately proud. It was the kind of gift a king might give to an ambassador, he

claimed. And indeed Beethoven was in many ways
the ambassador of the new and more romantic music
which the century about to begin was to produce.

On his return to Vienna from his concert tours,
with international fame new around him, and
having made the decision to concentrate mainly on
composing, Beethoven had to come to terms with
the question of patronage. He had been so wary of
it, after seeing its effects on Haydn and Mozart as
well as having experienced it in its best form under
Elector Maximilian Franz in Bonn. Reluctant
though he was to become the hireling or lackey of
some aristocratic family, he had always before him
the salutary example of Mozart, who, having
attempted to survive in Vienna as an independent
free-lance composer, had spent the last years of his
life in penury, accepting what commissions came
his way, and dying in abject poverty. He had met
and played for Mozart, as a novice before a master;
and now that master lay in an unmarked pauper's
grave. How was he himself to survive financially,
Beethoven wondered, especially if he spent less of
his time on the concert platform and more at
composition without a patron? His answer was to
have several patrons, but be beholden to none.

Prince Karl Lichnowsky, who had been his
landlord for a time, was a music-lover. Beethoven
had moved on to other lodgings, but their friendship had continued, and led to introductions to two
other aristocrats, in particular Baron von
Domanovecz, a court official and fine amateur
violinist, and Prince Franz Joseph von Lobkowitz,
who had a private orchestra. Beethoven was to find
himself always surrounded by high-ranking
admirers, whose support mainly took the form of
commissioning works for which they were
prepared to pay generously, and in payments of
'arrears' of money, which in fact they had already
paid him but pretended they had overlooked.
There was also no shortage of noble houses and
tables at which he was welcomed. That he often
preferred to eat alone at inns or live in inferior
lodgings of his choosing manifested his inherent
need of freedom; but it must have been some

comfort to know that assistance was being proffered, even if he did not necessarily choose to accept it. It is a tribute to those aristocratic music-lovers of Vienna that, although accustomed to command and be obeyed, they were prepared to accept his peculiar ways. Even before his pronounced eccentricities of later days appeared, Beethoven was headstrong and changeable in his relationships with friends. To the composer Hummel he sent one day a note calling him a dog and forbidding him to visit his house ever again. Next day he followed it with a letter in jocular, friendly vein, inviting Hummel to call soon.

Beethoven's friends needed to see the genius in him and not merely the rude exterior. His temperament was in fact in keeping with the *Zeitgeist* or spirit of the times in which he lived. As much as any product of fiction he represented the *Sturm und Drang* - storm and stress - movement of early Romanticism. Heroism meant dominating difficult circumstances, surviving in spite of opposition, no matter what the odds. It was characteristic of Beethoven all his life, and a view that was to sustain him through the almost incredible difficulties which were to beset him in the future.

As the eighteenth century drew to its close his future seemed bright and assured: established in Vienna; considered one of the premier pianists of Europe, and one of the most interesting young composers; enjoying the support of loyal if long-suffering aristocratic patrons; with a set of string quartets about to be published, three piano concertos written, more than a dozen mature piano sonatas and many chamber works completed; in reasonably good health, and with his two brothers now settled in the city in independent careers; all in all, Ludwig van Beethoven must have been looking towards the future with optimism.

Only one note of discord began to sound. From time to time, during applause following a concert or in the din of a crowded salon, Beethoven detected a curious sound in his ears, a sound like rushing water. He ignored it mainly; he certainly sought no medical advice for it, but it still persisted.

Little was he aware, at that most hopeful and promising nineteenth century's beginning, that, aged thirty, he was about to suffer the most appalling fate that could befall any musician - he was going deaf.

Love and Suffering

1800 – 1812

HAD BEETHOVEN DIED at thirty in 1800 it is unlikely he would be remembered today. One symphony, thought striking in its period, but the least revolutionary of his works; several sonatas for piano and various combinations of instruments; some trios and some songs; such would be the total of his achievement.

His health had never been in great shape. Even while in Bonn he had complained of colic and stomach pains. In Vienna he had chronic diarrhoea and suffered pain which often kept him in bed for several days. As this ailment grew worse the symptoms of deafness increased, and he and his doctors believed that it and the stomach complaint were related. 'It seems that this trouble was caused by the stomach complaint from which I was suffering before I left Bonn, but which has become much worse since I came to Vienna,' Beethoven wrote to his old friend Wegeler, now a doctor himself. Various physicians were consulted. One treated the ears with hot almond oil, while another recommended bathing in cold and warm water from the Danube. Although the stomach problem grew better from time to time, 'My ears buzz and hum day and night,' he wrote also to Wegeler, adding in a postscript that on no account was Wegeler's sister Lorchen to be told of this. Lorchen was not the only person from whom Beethoven tried to conceal his encroaching deafness; as a professional pianist

47

and teacher he had to hide it from his public. Besides the embarrassment he feared, and the threat that being deaf posed to his career, social gatherings with even a hum of conversation had begun to prove physically painful as all but the slightest noise was torture to him. 'I can tell you I lead a miserable life. For the last two years I have avoided going to any social functions because I cannot say to people "I am deaf...'

Although his deafness was progressive, and not total until the last ten years of his life, its effect threw Beethoven into indescribable gloom and caused a man already solitary in his habits to withdraw further into himself. His pupil and friend Ferdinand Ries was with him in the countryside near Vienna in the summer of 1802 and records how while they were walking in the fields together he remarked to Beethoven on the tune a shepherd was playing on his pipe. Beethoven had heard nothing, and though Ries tried to pass over the embarrassing mistake he noted that the incident brought on a great fit of depression. Faced with a future in which he would be cut off from normal social contact, and in which he would be unable to hear except in his mind the musical creations he was continually sketching and revising, faced too with physical illness of the most debilitating kind, Beethoven envisaged death, either from natural causes or by his own hand.

The summer of 1802 was spent in a despairing visit to the thermal baths at the peaceful village of Heiligenstadt, now a suburb of Vienna, and here, at the age of thirty-two, Beethoven composed what he believed to be his last will. In a document intended for his brothers Carl and Johann and written in Heiligenstadt on 6 October he set out his feelings with passionate ardour. The style, often rambling and confused, desperately struggling to communicate feelings he had only previously had in the depths of his mind, is as much an indication of his turmoil as the contents:

> O my fellow men, who consider me, or describe me as unfriendly, peevish or even misanthropic, how greatly do you wrong me. For you do not know the secret reason why I appear to you to be

so...just think, for the last six years I have been afflicted with an incurable complaint which has been made worse by incompetent doctors. From year to year my hopes of being cured have gradually been shattered, and finally I have been forced to accept the prospect of a permanent infirmity... Though fond of the distractions offered by society I was soon obliged to seclude myself and live in solitude... If I appear in company I am overcome by a burning anxiety, a fear that I am running the risk of letting people know of my condition. How humiliated I have felt if someone standing beside me heard the sound of a flute in the distance and I heard nothing, or if somebody heard a shepherd sing and again I heard nothing. Such experiences almost made me despair, and I was on the point of putting an end to my life. The only thing that held me back was my art. For indeed it seemed impossible to leave this world before I had produced all the works that I felt the urge to compose; and thus I have dragged on this miserable existence... Almighty God who look down into my innermost soul, you see into my heart and you know that it is filled with love for humanity and a desire to do good. Oh, my fellow men, when some day you read this statement, remember that you have done me wrong... I herewith nominate you both heirs to my small property...divide it honestly, live in harmony and help one another. Well, that is all. Joyfully I go to meet death - should it come before I have had an opportunity of developing my artistic gifts, then in spite of my hard fate it would still come too soon... Farewell, and when I am dead do not wholly forget me.

In a postscript of 10 October he added:

Thus I take leave of you - and, what is more, rather sadly - yes, the hope I cherished - the hope I brought here with me of being cured to a certain extent at any rate - that hope I now must abandon completely. As the autumn leaves fall and wither,

49

likewise - that hope has withered for me...Oh when, oh, when, Almighty God - shall I be able to hear and feel this echo again in the temple of nature and in contact with humanity -Never? - No! - Oh, that would be too hard.

Death did not come, either naturally or by suicide, and the Heiligenstadt Testament, as it came to be known, was not discovered until after his death and published in 1827. After writing it, Beethoven reconciled himself to his fate and squared up to it. He had agonised and come to accept, however sadly and reluctantly, that a life cut off from social intercourse was to be his, but he found sustaining power in his art. On his return to Vienna he remarked to a friend that he had thought over all his previous work and decided that from then on he would 'take a new road'. The Beethoven of the great central creative period was about to emerge, and its most visible symbol was to be the great Symphony No.3, the *Eroica*. From now on, Beethoven, living only for his art, was to abandon the conventions he had once followed, ignore what he found ready made, and follow his own internal promptings.

In 1804 he wrote to his Leipzig publishers, Breitkopf & Härtel, 'I have now finished a new grand symphony...the title of the symphony is *Bonaparte*... I think it will interest the musical public.' The subject of the symphony had been a hero of his since his youth. Napoleon Bonaparte seemed to represent all that was best in mankind asserting itself in the post-Revolutionary age in France. The French Revolution itself appealed to Beethoven as a concept from its beginning. With its ideas of Liberty, Equality and Brotherhood, it attracted his romantic imagination as a means of redressing the balance of power in Europe away from the aristocratic few and in favour of the oppressed many. Napoleon Bonaparte, child of this *Zeitgeist*, the Corsican soldier raised by his own talents to command the unstoppable armies of Revolutionary France, epitomised all that Beethoven saw as noble in man and the age. Consequently, the first major work of his 'new road' was a symphony, massive in construction and scale, which was to revolutionize the form in music as surely as Napoleon was to sweep away the Europe of the *ancien régime*.

The Symphony No.3 in E flat is a giant work in itself and a landmark in orchestral writing. Beethoven took the symphony orchestra of Haydn and added to its numbers, thereby being able to create volume, force and climax such as had never been known till then. The stately minuet movement was replaced with the more dynamic scherzo, and the theme and variations of the finale were on a scale of magnitude not before conceived in an orchestral work. The piece was almost twice as long as either of his first two symphonies and made unprecedented demands on players and listeners alike. The first performance was given semi-publicly in February 1805, but its true public première was in April, at the Theatre-an-der-Wien. It threw all who heard it into awed perplexity. One critic at that performance wrote:

> One fears that if Beethoven continues along this road the public will leave the hall with a feeling of unease and lassitude as a result of the strange superabundance of ideas and the incessant blowing of all instruments.

But Beethoven, determined to live only for the inner promptings of his art, took no notice of such critics. In the flood of compositions which were to follow in the next ten years in particular he stuck rigidly to his 'new road', and in the last ten years of his life that road became so unmapped and unfamiliar that it took almost a century before the rest of European music would find its way along it and endeavour to catch up with him.

How the 'Bonaparte Symphony' became the *Eroica* is a story as dramatic as the work itself. In 1804, with the final draft work in the hands of the copyist, Beethoven learned that his hero, his man from the people and of the people, had proclaimed himself Emperor of France. Beethoven's pupil Ries described his reaction:

> I was the first to announce to Beethoven that
> Napoleon had proclaimed himself Emperor. He
> flew into a rage and cried, 'Then he is nothing but
> an ordinary man! Now he will tread all human
> rights underfoot; he will think of nothing but his
> own ambition... he will raise himself up and
> become a tyrant.' He went over to the table, seized
> hold of the title page and tore it across and flung it
> to the ground. He rewrote the title page and the
> symphony was given a new name.

On other copies he scored out the name Bonaparte
and wrote *Sinfonia Eroica* in its place. None the
less, in Beethoven's mind the piece was always
linked with the idealised Napoleon, and when in
1821 he learned of the exiled and deposed
Emperor's death, he remarked 'I have already
written his funeral march', referring to the *Eroica's*
great second movement.

To a great extent the depression reflected in
Beethoven's diaries and in the Heiligenstadt Testament was caused by his realisation that with increasing deafness he must of necessity withdraw
from society, and from the company of women in
particular. While there is no doubt that he held his
'sacred art' above anything else in life, his attraction
to women was passionate and lifelong. He was far
from handsome or conventionally romantic: his
dark-skinned face was coarse and pitted from child-
hood smallpox, his thick black hair was often wildly
unkempt and his clothes frequently old and dirty, he
was clumsy and quick to rage and abuse, yet the
strength of his genius shone through his habitual
scowls, and he readily apologized for his bad
behaviour when he had calmed down. It made him
enigmatic and intriguing, and consequently fascina-
ting to women.

One of the first to whom he was romantically
attached was a pupil, the young Countess Giulietta
Guicciardi, whom he described as a 'dear, enchant-
ing girl'. Fond though she seems to have been of
him, she was beyond his reach and destined to
marry a man of her own social level, Count Robert
Gallenberg, and made her home with him in

Naples. Years later, finding herself in financial difficulties, she wrote to Beethoven asking for money
which was immediately dispatched to her. Some
years later still, while visiting Vienna, Giulietta tried
to see him, but he would not receive her; the wound
of her marriage to another had evidently not healed.

All his life Beethoven struggled with his sexual
passions. The noble, romantic idealist who prized
marriage and lifelong fidelity so highly struggled
against the human tendency to promiscuity. It was
once rumoured in Vienna and later widely believed
that he contracted syphilis, but this seems now
disproved. The medicines based on mercury which
appeared among his many doctors' prescriptions
were probably to ease his continual intestinal ail-
ments and quite unrelated to similar drugs used in
the treatment of syphilis.

In 1805 he fell in love with yet another of his piano
pupils, Therese von Brunswick. Beethoven had
been cordially received by the Brunswick family
since his arrival in Vienna and was a friend of
Therese's brother Franz and married sister Josephine. Friend of this notable Hungarian family he
may have been, but Therese's mother was determined that he should not become a member of it.
Perhaps she recognized that he was also in love with
Josephine, who was separated from her husband
and lived at her mother's with her children. Both
Therese and her sister rejected him, but his deep
love for both endured and was manifested in some of
the works of this period, notably the Fourth
Symphony, the Sixth (the *Pastoral*), and the intense
Piano Sonatas Op.53 (*Waldstein*) and Op.57
(*Appassionata*). Although Beethoven's ideal world
was one in which genius took precedence over
wealth, rank or title, the world of Viennese society
thought differently. An eccentric genius with only
the income from his compositions to rely on was not
considered a fit marriage partner for a daughter of
Viennese nobility, and by 1810 all hopes of marriage
with either sister had been crushed, though not
without stormy resistance from him. That Beethoven never forgot Therese can be seen from the fact
that only a year before his death he still kept in a

secret drawer a portrait of her on which she had written 'To the unequalled genius, to the great artist and a worthy man.' She never married, devoting her life to good works, and Josephine married another man for the sake of her children's stability, no doubt a wiser if less adventurous choice.

Another young woman in Beethoven's life was Bettina von Brentano, a German-Italian friend of Goethe's, with girlish looks and high spirits to match. As a poetess, she understood Beethoven's intense sadness at the collapse of his hopes for the Brunswick sisters, and set out to fill the void. She was talented and interesting enough to be admired by such disparate persons as Goethe, Liszt and, later, King Louis of Bavaria, while the composer and writer E.T.A. Hoffmann likened her singing voice to the finest of organs. To Goethe, Bettina wrote of Beethoven, 'near him I forget the world and even you… I think I am not wrong in believing him to be far ahead of modern civilisation.' Her penchant for exaggeration has become well known, and it is regarded as highly unlikely that Beethoven's attachment to her was as deep as she cared to make out: he saw her as possessive and demanding and kept at a shrewd distance. She married the romantic poet Arnim.

Another family with which Beethoven became intimate during this emotionally turbulent period were the cultured and musically-gifted Malfattis, whose head, Joseph Malfatti, prominent in Viennese medical circles, became his physician. Beethoven wrote, 'I am so happy when I am with them… I feel somehow that all that the wicked people have inflicted on my soul could be cured by the Malfattis.' There were two daughters, Therese and Anna, both extremely beautiful. It was the 18-year-old Therese who engaged Beethoven's fancy and even caused him to tidy up his appearance. She was witty, lively and gifted, a singer and a fine pianist, just the sort for him. He became infatuated, to the point of getting a friend to put out feelers towards her family about his prospects of marrying her. Her family were horrified, and, anyway, she had only been playing with him. Predictably, she subsequently married a nobleman.

Other women flitted through Beethoven's life, all arousing in him physical passion and emotional turmoil which are reflected in his great 'middle period' works. There was Amalie Sebald, proud-looking with huge penetrating dark eyes and the long fine neck which contributed to her aristocratic appearance, who was among his favourite singers and performers of his works. There was Rachel Levin, who later married the soldier and poet Ense. And there was Dorothea von Enturann, a pianist who became a notable interpreter of his works. At the height of his creative drive it is scarcely surprising that Beethoven fell in love to some degree with most young women of beauty and charm whom he encountered; but always within him there was that longing for the settled, idealised marriage he so highly prized in others, and which he was never to have.

He seems to have had at least one much deeper romance than all the others. After his death, letters were found to an unknown woman, his *Unsterbliche Geliebte*, 'Immortal Beloved', which proclaim a depth of passion and an attachment far in excess of that shown in any of the letters he wrote to any but her. It may be that the letters were returned to him or that he never sent them, but compared to the known love letters he wrote their tone is ardent and sincere and well beyond mere flirtatiousness.

July 6, morning

My angel, my all, my very self. - Only a few words today, and, what is more, written in pencil (and with your pencil) - I shall not be in my rooms here until tomorrow...Can our love endure without sacrifices, without our demanding everything from one another; can you alter the fact that you are not wholly mine, that I am not wholly yours? Dear God, look at Nature in all her beauty and set your heart at rest about what must be...

Ludwig van Beethoven

Monday evening, July 6th.

You are suffering, you, my most precious one...
Oh, where I am you are with me - I will see to it
that you and I, that I can live with you. What a
life!!!! as it is now!!!!... I weep when I think that
you will not receive the first news of me until
Saturday - however much you love me - my love
for you is even greater - but never conceal yourself
from me... Is not our love truly founded in
heaven - and, what is more, as strongly cemented
as the firmament of heaven?

Good morning, on July 7th

Even when I am in bed my thoughts rush to you,
my eternally beloved, now and then joyfully, and
then sadly, waiting to know whether Fate will
hear our prayer - To face life I must live alto-
gether with you or never see you... no other
woman can ever possess my heart -never -
never - Oh God, why must one be separated
from one who is so dear... Your love has made me
both the happiest and unhappiest of
mortals - at my age I now need stability and
regularity in my life - can this coexist with our
relationship?... Be calm - love me -Today -
yesterday - what tearful longing for you -for
you - you - my life - my all - all good wishes to
you - Oh, do continue to love me - never mis-
judge your lover's most faithful heart.

ever yours
ever mine
ever ours
L.

No one has ever discovered to whom this letter was
sent or for whom it was intended: Therese von
Brunswick is perhaps the speculative favourite,
although her sister Josephine's name has been
much mentioned, too. It shows clearly the struggle
Beethoven put up for a love and stability which
would make passing flirtations and occasional

affairs unnecessary. It shows too that he had to have all or nothing in such a marriage. His standards in women as in his art were the highest and his demands exacting. Fate seems to have decreed that he fall in love with women who were unobtainable, and it may well be that no woman could have come up to his ideal.

A great artist seldom attains his professional ideals, either. In trying to fulfil his genius, Beethoven was able to draw on the emotions of unrequited love, and his work was thus enriched, even if his personal life was not. His emotions are bared through his immortal music, though the identity of the 'Immortal Beloved' remains unknowable, perhaps for ever.

Master Works

1804 – 1809

THE IDEAL WIFE may have eluded Beethoven in life but he was able to realize one in his music. From his letters we know that his imagination had been caught by a French story by Jean Nicolas Bouilly of how, during the Terror in Revolutionary France, a wife had rescued her husband from prison through disguising herself as a man in order to gain access to him. Bouilly had been Prosecutor General of the Tours Revolutionary Tribunal and had based his story on an actual happening elsewhere in the country. The theme of captivity and liberation, the triumph of freedom over tyranny, and the self-sacrifice of a faithful wife for a husband, appealed at once to Beethoven, who spent the whole of 1804 engaged on expressing it in music.

He used a high moral standpoint in judging texts sent to him for possibly setting to music, and would only consider those he felt to be sufficiently noble or at least worthy. He considered *Don Giovanni* a theme unworthy of Mozart's music, and *Cosi fan Tutte* positively distasteful in the way it made light of marital fidelity. For Beethoven, an elevating libretto could give rise to appropriate musical themes, but a text he found ignoble left him uninspired. Therefore when his friends urged him to tackle an opera it was fortuitous that he had been offered Bouilly's appeal-ing book, *Leonora, ou l'amour conjugal*.

The story of *Fidelio*, as his only opera came to be called, is straightforward. Florestan, a liberal oppressed by a totalitarian régime, finds himself in the prison governed by his arch enemy Don Pizarro. Pizarro knows, though Florestan does not, that the old order has been overthrown and that a new enlightened monarch is sending a minister, Don Fernando, to enfranchise all prisoners taken in the time of oppression, and he determines to murder Florestan and bury him in the cellars of the prison before the minister can arrive to free him. Before this, however, Leonora, Florestan's wife, disguised as a young man with the assumed name Fidelio, has ingratiated herself into the chief jailer's family and become his assistant. In this capacity she is able to accompany him into her husband's cell when he goes to dig a grave for Florestan on Pizarro's orders. Florestan does not recognize his wife in disguise and begs for food from her. She has only just given him some when Pizarro sweeps in and orders the jailer and his assistant out so that he can stab Florestan to death. In a dramatic dénouement Leonora leaps between Pizarro's knife and her husband, drawing a pistol to protect him and herself and revealing her true identity. Pizarro is stopped in his tracks and unable to move. At this moment a fanfare from the tower announces the arrival of the minister, Don Fernando, and signals all the prisoners' release. The opera ends with Pizarro's being led off, and a jubilant chorus from the prisoners, their wives and, not least, the united Florestan and Leonora.

What this account of the story lacks is what makes *Fidelio* the ever-popular and constantly-played masterpiece it is: Beethoven's music. Although the work is in form totally conventional in the pattern of nineteenth-century Italian opera, but with the text in German, as had been Mozart's last opera, *Die Zauberflöte (The Magic Flute)*, Beethoven was able to write music of a degree which lifts it to the level of a dramatic oratorio: the beautiful and poignant opening trio in which Leonora asks of the fate of the prisoner deep in the bowels of the castle; the inexpressibly moving chorus from the prisoners when they are allowed a brief glimpse of light; the tension of the dungeon scene climaxing in Leonora's cry at Pizarro with his raised knife, 'Töt' erst sein Weib!'

(First kill his wife!); the ecstasy of the reunited husband and wife, 'O namenlose Freude! Mein Mann an meiner Brust!' (Oh joy beyond expressing! My husband in my arms!); and the final seemingly endless chorus of rejoicing in freedom, 'Heil sei dem Tag, Heil sei der Stunde!':

> Hail to the day, hail to the hour
> So long awaited and so long denied,
> When justice and mercy
> Has unlocked the gates of death!

Such masterly writing transforms the story from a run-of-the mill melodrama into opera of the highest level and a piece to stir all who value, as its creator did, the great eternal values of fidelity and freedom.

With unfortunate irony, the first presentation of the work, scheduled for mid-October 1805, co-incided with the surrender of the Austrian army to Napoleon at Ulm. Bouilly had changed the country and the century in writing his story, so as not to seem to be commenting on the conduct of the régime he served, and with the French about to occupy Vienna the same sort of problem faced *Fidelio*. The opening was postponed and judicious cuts were made. Napoleon entered the city in triumph on 13 November, to take up residence at the Schönbrunn Palace, from which the royal family had fled. When *Fidelio* had its première at the Theater-an-der-Wien on the 20th the scant audience comprised mainly officers of the occupying force, who let it be known that they liked neither the Germanic setting nor Beethoven's music for what, to do them some justice, was an excessively long work, under-rehearsed and poorly sung.

It was not until nine years later that the shortened and much-revised version at last gained acclaim at a performance at Vienna's Kärntnertortheater, on 23 May 1814. By then it had had four different over-tures composed for it. The three discarded ones are familiar as the *Leonora* Overtures Nos.1 - 3, *Leonora* having been Beethoven's original preferred title for the opera. The fourth one could not be used at this new première, for the composer had only finished it in the early hours of that morning and fallen into exhausted sleep. He was discovered too late for any rehearsal, and the overture *The Ruins of Athens* was played instead. It detracted nothing from the success; nor did the spectacle of *Kapellmeister* Umlauf directing cast and orchestra from behind Beethoven's back when 'his ardour often rushed him out of time', which few people knew was attributable to his deafness.

The opera played in Leipzig, Prague and Berlin and was rapturously received there, too. Although it represented a milestone in his popularity, Beethoven was never entirely satisfied with his only opera; his intense feeling for its theme seemed to him incapable of full expression. Yet it still represents the greatest opera of the *Sturm und Drang* period, and for many music lovers has no parallel.

Knowing how Haydn and Mozart had fared under the traditional patronage system, Beethoven was always guarded in his attitude to those who were paying him, and often downright rude. After Count Waldstein had come Prince Lobkowitz, in whose palace the *Eroica* had first been performed, and in 1806 a breach developed between these two which, though short-lived, was a violent one. Beethoven spent the summer of that year on Lobkowitz's estate in Silesia, composing, among other works, the Violin Concerto in D. In September the Prince was also playing host to some French nobles, and it seems that he instructed Beethoven somewhat too sharply to 'make some music' for his guests. Feeling that he was being spoken to like a servant, or at best had to earn his keep by performing at his master's whim, Beethoven flew into a rage, roaring at Lobkowitz, 'There are plenty of princes, but there is only one Beethoven!' He promptly packed and left the house. Later he was to write to the Prince, 'Prince, who you are you owe to your birth, but what I am I owe to myself.'

Although the general opinion of Beethoven was that he was arrogant and insufferable, such was the respect in which his genius was held that his friends and patrons were always prepared to overlook his eccentrically independent behaviour. The story is told, though it may be apocryphal, that on the occasion when Beethoven met Goethe they walked in the park at Teplitz and in the course of their stroll chanced upon the royal family coming in the opposite direction. Goethe broke off his conversation, stepped aside and bowed deeply. Beethoven kept on and walked through the royal party. What is certain is that he reported of Goethe: 'Goethe likes the atmosphere of the Court too much; more than is becoming to him as a poet.'

A meticulous and slow composer who worked on several pieces simultaneously and was constantly in the process of revising all he wrote, Beethoven could not support himself by his income from publishers, even though his works sold well. Had he not found support from friends he could never have devoted so much of his time to composition and would have been forced to take piano pupils, which he did in the case of the specially talented, but which he hated in principle as time-consuming and unrewarding. One engagement he fortunately did not refuse, in 1806, was to give lessons in the piano and composition to the Emperor's younger brother, the Archduke Rudolph of Austria. This civilised man, only twenty, had taken holy orders and was destined to become Cardinal and Archbishop of Olmütz; he was also destined to become Beethoven's most loyal supporter. In him Beethoven found great natural talent and considerable musical taste, and a bond that was more of affection than courteous regard grew up between them. In time the composer was to dedicate to him the *Archduke* Piano Trio Op.97, the Sonata Op.81a *(Les Adieux)*, the Piano Concertos Nos.4 and 5, the *Grosse Fuge* String Quartet, Op.133, and the magnificient *Missa Solemnis.* Special arangements were made at the palace in Vienna for Beethoven's music lessons with Prince Rudolph; he was able to enter and leave by a special door and many forms of protocol were dispensed with. On the Archduke's personal instructions Court etiquette was waived for him, and the master in return immortalised this royal patron through some of his finest works.

Other rich and noble men were of aid to Beethoven

at this time by commissioning a variety of works. Count Oppersdorf received the dedication of the Fourth Symphony, and Prince Nicholas Esterhazy, of the family which had been Haydn's life-long patrons, commissioned the Mass in C major in 1807. Count Rasumowsky, the fabulously wealthy Russian ambassador who employed a private string quartet under the leadership of Beethoven's violinist friend Ignaz Schuppanzigh, commissioned the three quartets Op.59, composed in 1805-6, which today are known by Rasumowsky's name. These were all genuine music lovers who cherished Beethoven's genius and were determined to keep him in funds. Even so, in 1808 an offer was made to him which was sufficiently tempting to make him give it more serious consideration than he had to any similar offer before, and caused his friends to rally anxiously round in a determined move to keep him in Vienna.

Napoleon Bonaparte's conquests in Europe had enabled him to set up his family in kingdoms throughout its length and breadth. He made his youngest brother, Jerome, King of Westphalia, in an effort to establish a buffer kingdom between Prussia and France. In 1808 an approach was made on behalf of King Jerome to Beethoven to invite him to become *Kapellmeister* at his Court in Cassel. The terms of the offer invited him to name an annual salary, and placed no restraints on the type of composition he would undertake or the time he would have to spend on court work. It is a testament to Beethoven's international standing at this time that these unheard-of conditions were offered to him: no other composer would have commanded such terms.

He was feeling restless and discontented. In spite of his relative security, he was not above referring to his patrons as 'princely rabble' and complaining that Vienna was full of his 'private enemies', namely the critics who failed to praise his music, outlandishly modern to many ears and often badly performed - another cause for him to grumble. He was also jealous of his brother Johann, now a rich chemist and businessman, able to sign a letter to him 'Johann Beethoven, Property Owner', which provoked him to term himself 'Brain Owner' in reply. And he wanted time to compose an opera a year, and be paid sufficient retainer to enable him to concentrate absolutely on it. This proposal was not accepted by those other supposed enemies of his, the promoters of music in Vienna. He had hinted that he might be more appreciated abroad, and now this kingly offer had come his way.

His decision to accept it seemed confirmed by the poor reception given to a 'farewell concert' which he had organized in the Theater-an-der-Wien in December 1808. It included the 5th and 6th Symphonies, the G Major Piano Concerto, the *Choral Fantasia* for piano and orchestra, and some songs. The performance was bad, and the new work being given its première was scarcely considered by the critics. It has since become established as one of the most-performed works in the symphonic repertoire: 'Beethoven's Fifth'.

He tested out the proposal from Westphalia with a request for an annual stipend of 600 gold ducats for life - a huge sum for a composer of the time - and, to everyone's astonishment, it was agreed.

He prepared to shake the ungrateful dust of Vienna off his shoes. But his fame was too great in his adopted city for it to let him go so easily. The regard he was held in by his friends and the general public was far warmer than he had acknowledged, and certainly too great for them to accept his leaving. A petition was put around the music-loving nobility in the city asking for contributions to a fund to supply Beethoven with a regular income. In the end three of the 'princely rabble', Archduke Rudolph, Prince Lobkowitz (whose rift with Beethoven had long since been overcome), and Prince Ferdinand Kinsky agreed that together they would guarantee him an annual pension of 4,000 florins on condition that he remain in Vienna. On 1 March 1809, to their everlasting credit, these three men signed a contract, part of which read,

Since it has been demonstrated that only a man who is free of all material cares can devote himself wholly to his art, the undersigned have decided to place Herr Ludwig van Beethoven in a position where he will be free from all the miserable obstacles which might inhibit the full play of his genius...

Though it was in subsequent years to be lessened when the Austrian currency was devalued, and also to be the grounds of a lawsuit by Beethoven against the estate of Prince Lobkowitz, this income brought him security at a time when he most needed it, enabled him to consent to remain in the city which he had certainly never really wanted to leave, and yet allowed his notorious independence to stay uncompromised. The patrons felt they had achieved their wish and Beethoven felt free to follow his own course, financially secure.

Posterity has much reason to thank those perceptive young patrons, for the years through which their difficult beneficiary was passing were among the most creative of his life. They saw the emergence of Piano Concertos Nos.4 and 5; the Symphonies Nos.4 to 8; the Violin Concerto; *Fidelio*, and the great overture and incidental music to Goethe's heroic drama *Egmont;* a host of piano sonatas, string quartets, other chamber music in various combinations, and many songs.

Of this list unquestionably the most significant part of his output were the symphonies. While the Fourth might be said to be a complete counterpart to the huge *Eroica*, being smaller and closer in tone to the works of Mozart, his Fifth represents a revolutionary step in the form. It has not only been his most popular symphony, but for most people is his most characteristic work. It never loses its drive from those first four notes which down the years have always been identified with overcoming seemingly impossible odds. (During the Second World War, British broadcasts to occupied European countries began with the three rapid notes folowed by the long one, as an identification and also as a renewal of courage for peoples under the heel of a régime which

Beethoven would have found an abomination.)

Asked how he had come to conceive the opening bars of this work and if they had any extra-musical significance for him, Beethoven told his friend Schindler that the phrase represented 'how destiny knocks on the door'. Destiny or fate at that time seemed to Beethoven to come with a hostile knock indeed. 'Very great and very long' was how one critic described the Fifth, which contemporary orchestral players found very difficult. Discerning hearers, though perhaps not able to 'understand' it, as we still say of revolutionary new work, could at least tell that it was something stupendous. Although it follows the classical form of the symphony perfectly it was the brusqueness and directness of its musical phrases which stunned its first hearers. To add to its dramatic qualities Beethoven introduced a double-bassoon, trombones and a piccolo into the scoring, adding weight at one end of the register and brilliance at the other, with amazing climactic effect in the breathtaking last bars of the finale.

Tending to work on the symphonies in pairs, Beethoven divided the differing sides of his personality between each two. Thus the odd-numbered ones are longer, very driving and more dramatic, while the even-numbered ones are more lyrical and generally more light-hearted. This is the case with the Sixth, which was composed more or less alongside the Fifth, and is the only one of Beethoven's to have a 'programme'; that is, the only one to which a broadly narrative 'story' can be fitted. He called the work his *Pastoral* Symphony, and although at the head of the score he wrote 'Expression of sensation rather than painting', each movement has a character of its own, reflecting aspects of the countryside which Beethoven loved so much.

The first movement, 'Awakening of feelings on going into the countryside', begins simply and builds up into a great swelling hymn of joy at the wonder of nature, and this is continued into the slow movement. The scherzo represents a peasant dance interrupted by a storm, vividly created in musical terms by deep double-bass tremulants and piccolo interjections to represent lightning flashes. The storm over, the shepherd calls his flock with a flute tune of haunting beauty which Beethoven takes up and makes into a theme and variations of immense scale. The whole work is a great statement of joy in nature and shows better than anything that the composer who knew only too well the buffets of fate as represented in his Fifth Symphony knew equally how they might be overcome by effort of will. It is amazing to think that the work, a great song from beginning to end, could have been produced by a sick man, rapidly going deaf.

Beethoven's illnesses have never been fully understood. The state of medical knowledge at the time was such that no definite diagnosis was ever put forward. His constant stomach cramps and chronic diarrhoea often forced him to bed for days on end and induced him to try bizarre cures. His deafness was for a time thought to stem from his intestinal disorders - the syphilis theory is often advanced in this connection. Driven by the urge to create, but prevented by illness from working, he was also subject to fits of depression, and at such times he was almost impossible to calm down or help. Only his music sustained him.

In spite of constant illness he was able to complete another two complementary symphonies in 1812, the Seventh and Eighth. Unlike the other odd-numbered symphonies, the Seventh is not intensely dramatic in tone; it is a great, vast dance. The composer Wagner was later to call it 'the apotheosis of the dance' because of its powerful rhythms based on dance time. In typical contrast the Eighth symphony is lighthearted and whimsical in the spirit of a peasant celebration, close in tone to that of the *Pastoral*. Beethoven seems to have had a special fondness for the Eighth, which he called his 'little symphony' to distinguish it from its longer companions. Paradoxically, his public, accustoming itself to the powerful and dynamically aggressive style which had at first seemed so hard to accept, took less to this lighter work than its composer anticipated. Critics then and now have found its humour too light and in some cases its earthiness too lumpen. It is still, with the first two of his symphonies, less played than the others.

Though many people would hold that Beethoven's greatest works were to come much later in his life, products of what is regarded as his 'third period', and bearing in mind his bad health and hearing, the assurance he displayed during these middle years of his career, and the speedy facility with which he worked, are remarkable: perhaps the more so in the light of the fact that for several years before this time Napoleon's forces, having defeated the Austrian army at Austerlitz, were again advancing on Vienna.

War and Family Trials

1809 – 1820

IN HIS SWEEP EASTWARD Napoleon determined once and for all to disarm the Austrian capital and force it to surrender. In an exemplary display of fire power, the suburbs of Vienna were bombarded by French artillery.

Though never intended to destroy much of the city, the impact of the shelling was astounding. The Court and nobility fled for their country estates, leaving social life at a standstill. Without his patrons to appeal to or his fashionable followers to attend the concerts of his works, Beethoven's income was greatly reduced. More than that, the sound of the guns was a torment to a man trying to preserve the last vestiges of his hearing on which his profession so much depended, but which was now all but totally gone. According to his pupil, Ries, he went to great lengths to avoid the noise: 'He spent most of his time in a cellar of his brother Carl's house, where he buried his head in pillows so as not to hear the cannon.' After an heroic but fated attempt to defend themselves, the Viennese surrendered, and in October 1809 the Treaty of Schönbrunn was signed. The city was still in a state of shock, but for Beethoven at least the end of the bombardment brought relief from pain.

But the city was now to suffer a different kind of assault. With French soldiers stationed in it, supplies of all kinds, and of food in particular, began to run short. Since supply was at its lowest as demand was at its height, prices for what was available soared and inflation hit the city so badly that the government had to devalue the currency. The result of this for Beethoven was that his income of 4,000 florins a year was reduced in effect to 1,600. Characteristically, the Archduke Rudolph gave instructions that his share of the payment was to increase in proportion to its loss of value, but Prince Lobkowitz was himself in financial difficulties and unable to pay anything at all towards Beethoven's support. Prince Kinsky, who had agreed to increase his share, was accidentally killed just before he was able to put the decision into effect. It is not greatly to Beethoven's credit, though the effect of total upheaval on a now completely deaf man who cared more for the continuance of his 'divine art' than for anything else must not be discounted, that his reaction to these tragic events was to take legal action against the estates of Kinsky and Lobkowitz. The latter, who suffered much in his life from Beethoven's quick temper, wrote to the Archduke, 'I have reason to be anything but satisfied with the behaviour of Beethoven towards me'; but he continued a patron of his until his death in 1816.

All this time Beethoven was working on the last and greatest of his piano concertos, the Fifth in E flat, known as the *Emperor* because of its magnificence and scale. The sweeping nature of the concerto well echoed the valiant attempts of the Austrians to repel the French, and in the margin of the score Beethoven scribbled war-like words such as 'Attack!' and 'Victory!'

On the last day of May 1809 the 77-year-old Joseph Haydn died. Although the city was under occupation, many of its population, including Beethoven, attended his funeral. Haydn had achieved much, transforming the symphony and string quartet almost single-handedly from slight affairs into major modes of musical expression, and Beethoven never lost his reverence for him. Although it coincided with a particularly bad period of ill-health for Beethoven he insisted on turning out to follow the coffin of his sometime friend and teacher.

Life, however, continued. Beethoven was still

subject to the same passions as he had always been, and the letters to the 'Immortal Beloved' date from 1812. Family affairs also took more of his time than he would have liked. In October 1812 he rushed to Linz to try to prevent his brother Johann from marrying his current mistress. The wealthy 'Property Owner' had been living in very close conjunction with his housekeeper, Therese Obermeyer, and at last intended to make an honest woman of her. Beethoven, with his romantic views on marriage, was appalled by the situation and resolved to prevent it. When Johann refused to be swayed by his brother's advice Ludwig attempted to take out a legal injunction which would force Therese, whom he detested and called 'the dumpling', to leave the city. Johann pre-empted his brother's actions by promptly marrying Therese, thereby settling the matter and leaving the 'Brain Owner' to return to Vienna in a rage. He was never to forgive Johann or his 'dumpling'.

A more pleasant event of 1812 was the meeting which took place through the influence of Bettina von Brentano between Beethoven and Johann Wolfgang von Goethe. Beethoven had for some time been composing incidental music for Goethe's two-act play *Egmont*, an heroic work to some extent based on fact and with certain superficially suggestive parallels with *Fidelio*. The courtly 62-year-old poet found the 41-year-old musician 'too wild and untamed' for his taste, but when he heard Beethoven play the piano he was astonished by his power and virtuosity. 'His talent amazed me,' he admitted to a friend. The story is told that as the two strolled through a park Goethe became irritated at the number of people who raised their hats to them and bowed to him. 'Your Excellency shouldn't trouble yourself,' Beethoven commented; 'it may be that these bows are directed at me only.'

It would be pleasant to record that their meeting brought forth joint projects, but nothing at all came of it. Beethoven found Goethe too aware of the niceties of social conduct, and Goethe found Beethoven almost madly eccentric. Years later when, at eighty, he met the young Mendelssohn in

Weimar, Beethoven was not a topic he was prepared to go into with the intensely curious young composer. The coda to this anecdote, however, is that after Mendelssohn had played for him a piano transcription of the first movement of Beethoven's Fifth Symphony, Goethe was so visibly affected by it that he refused further company and went home pale and alone. The poet of the *Sturm und Drang* movement could not but recognize in Beethoven the most potent voice of the age, even if he found the embodiment of it too rough for his sophisticated tastes.

With the defeat of Napoleon at Leipzig in 1814 Europe was once again in upheaval, and it was decided to convene the international Congress of Vienna at which new treaties and boundaries could be drawn up. Every power in Europe, great and small, sent its representatives, and the winter of 1814-1815 saw such a series of noble and royal visitors as the city had never before known.

Beethoven had struck up a friendship with the pianist and inventor Johann Maelzel, the developer of the metronome from a design he appears to have stolen from someone else. More his own was a mechanical orchestra, known as the 'Panharmonicon' and comprising pins and rotating brass cylinders, tubes, reeds, percussion, and other devices, enabling it to simulate a wide range of instruments. As an avid publicist for his own wares he conceived the idea of approaching Beethoven to compose a special 'symphony' for his device, thereby ensuring a fortune for them both. Ever aware of his tight financial circumstances, Beethoven accepted and composed a piece which was subsequently named the *Battle* Symphony by its English publisher. That Maelzel and Beethoven were bound to quarrel - as Beethoven did with everyone sooner or later, particularly if money was involved - was inevitable from the outset. However, this *Battle* Symphony, representing in musical terms the Duke of Wellington's victory over the French at Vitoria, was later to be fully orchestrated by the composer and made use of to bring him to full prominence during the Congress.

To advertise the mechanical player Beethoven had arranged a charity concert from whose proceeds a large amount would be donated to relieve the condition of the wounded soldiers of the victorious armies. When the concert proved a success, as Beethoven never doubted it would, subsequent performances would be staged for his own benefit. The idea caught the imagination of the public and musicians of Vienna and for once Beethoven's music was played by an orchestra made up of the leading instrumentalists of the day and listened to by a well-wishing audience. To make up the programme Beethoven included his Seventh Symphony, a Choral Cantata, and a celebratory choral work entitled *Der glorreiche Augenblick* (The Glorious Moment).

On 29 October 1814 an audience of 6,000, including many ambassadors and crowned heads, heard this concert and were rapturous in their applause. Beethoven had caught the spirit of relief and jubilation which followed the fall of Napoleon. The *Battle* Symphony known at the time as *Wellington's Victory*, cannot be described as one of his great works by any standards, but it was topical, loud and exciting, making use of such rousing tunes as 'Rule Britannia', cannon shots and much beating of drums, and brought Beethoven instant international and public success. He was introduced to many of the notable people attending the concert.

Through the Archduke Rudolph he was presented to the Tsar and Tsarina of Russia, and on 25 January 1815, the Tsarina's birthday, a Beethoven concert was given in the Rittersaal before all the assembled royalty. It was a glorious occasion, yet in another way a poignant one, for it was Beethoven's last public appearance as a pianist. He was now so totally deaf that he got completely out of time with the orchestra, and the concerto was a fiasco. However, the concert as a whole was a great financial success, and on the strength of his current popularity Beethoven had a revival of *Fidelio* mounted to popular and critical acclaim.

Beethoven's star was never to be higher. His income from concert performances of his works was never greater than at this time. From the many royal personages he met he received gifts and valuable presents, and he was made an 'honorary citizen' of Vienna. Publishers vied for his works. A commission arrived from London from the newly founded Philharmonic Society offering £75 for three 'concert overtures': he duly obliged, but the works he provided were not new ones, and were not well received. But as ever in Beethoven's life, his respite from struggles was to be a brief one. In February 1815 Napoleon escaped from Elba and made another attempt to assert himself by force. The Congress in Vienna was hastily disbanded and pleasure gave way to anxiety. Beethoven's old troubles came flooding back. Maelzel had had the *Battle* copied and was claiming it as his own property and playing it on his mechanical contraption without paying Beethoven his fees as composer. This resulted in legal action, which dragged on until 1817.

In the personal sphere, Beethoven's brother Carl had died of consumption on 15 November 1815. Beethoven's relations with his brothers and their families was always a curious one. Both had made unconventional and, to his mind, wrongheaded marriages, in which he interfered to a degree which might almost have been designed to alienate himself from them; yet Carl named him as guardian to his son, Karl, aged nine. Unfortunately, in a codicil, Carl also named the boy's mother, Johanna, whom Beethoven detested for her loose morals and nicknamed 'Queen of the Night'. She had married Carl when four months pregnant with his son. He once had her arrested for embezzling his money, for which she was kept under house arrest for a month, and during his last illness she was carrying on an affaire with a man by whom she had a child soon after Carl's death. Johanna moved in the more raffish of Vienna's artistic circles. Beethoven wrote of her: 'Last night the Queen of the Night was at the Artists' Ball till 3 a.m., exposing not only her mental but *her physical nakedness* - it was whispered that she would sell herself for 20 gulden!' Not surprisingly, he determined to dispute her joint guardianship in the courts, never realising how costly and protracted that would prove.

That he was fond of the boy Karl, and came to feel a fanatical devotion for him, is undoubted. It is equally certain that he himself was totally unsuited to be the guardian of a lad of this age. Karl's mother may have been promiscuous and foolish, but Beethoven was a bachelor of forty-four, now suffering from serious ill-health, stone deaf, of eccentric habits, and devoted entirely to his 'holy art'. That the first years of his guardianship, with the ensuing court cases, were the least productive in musical output of his career, is hardly surprising in view of his attempts to turn himself from his bachelor eccentricity into 'the natural father of this boy', as he styled and thought of himself. An account from a few years earlier of Beethoven's apartment in Vienna by the French Baron de Tremont, who had visited him there, may serve to draw a graphic picture of the domestic environment into which he proposed to introduce his nephew:

> Picture to yourself the extreme of dirt and disorder: pools of water decorating the floor, and a rather ancient grand piano on which dust competed for room with sheets of paper or printed notes. Under it - I do not exaggerate - an unemptied chamber pot...most of the chairs were decorated with clothes and with dishes full of the remains of the previous day's supper.

However unsuited he was to the role of substitute father, as soon as his brother's will was known Beethoven took possession of Karl and packed him off to a boarding school run by the del Rio family, the daughter of which, Fanny, adored Beethoven with a longing that does not seem to have been reciprocated. Beethoven was determined that Karl should have a good moral and social education and should turn into a first-rate musician or classical scholar. His letters to the del Rios show it, but there is something rather spinsterly and maiden-auntish in their tone, concerning himself incongruously with the trivia of the boy's life. He wrote to Karl himself, 'Put on a pair of underpants or bring them with you so that you can put them on immediately after your bath, in case the weather turns colder again.' The boy disliked the school, however, and Beethoven eventually had to take him away from it, though still nursing grand ambitions for him, even hoping that he might enter him at the Theresianum, a school exclusively educating sons of the nobility founded by the Empress Maria Theresa, and the equivalent in social standing of the great English public schools.

Karl was torn between the natural affections of a boy for his mother, no matter what she may have been like, and dutiful respect for his bizarre though entirely well-meaning uncle. Living with Beethoven, with housekeepers coming and going by the week as Beethoven's suspicions of their fraudulence or gossiping grew worse than ever, he was not well looked after physically. There are revealing entries in the conversation notebooks in which all communication with the now totally deaf Beethoven had to be conducted in writing: Karl wrote the lines, but Bethoven's responses can only be conjectured:

> I don't know where all these lice come from!
> But it's healthy to have lice.
> On each foot I have five corns.
> He cut open my chilblained toe today.

Beethoven constantly brought up the subject of how his late brother had accepted money from him without the intention of repaying it, while reference to the boy's mother drew from her disgusted brother-in-law streams of invective and curses far in excess of any he used about his many real and imaginary adversaries. It is little wonder that Karl grew up to be a confused young man.

Johanna was expressly forbidden to see her son, as Beethoven was always adamant in emphasizing to his teachers. It says much for her that she was prepared to go to great lengths to visit Karl, even as far as disguising herself as a man. When Beethoven realized that she was still managing to see Karl he took his usual recourse and went to law against her. Between 1816 and 1820 he was constantly engaged in the tussle, gaining an injunction which forbade

Johanna to see her son without Beethoven's prior consent. That he did all this for the boy's well-being as he saw it is clear from his diaries, in which he prays for God's forgiveness if he should 'hurt the widow', but adds that it was all being done 'for dear Karl's sake'.

'What will people say - they will take me for a tyrant,' he confided to a close woman friend at the time. With that realization he allowed a truce in their battle in 1817. At the time he was working on the great Piano Sonata Op.106 (the *Hammerklavier*) and negotiating with the Philharmonic Society of London, who, despite their disappointment with the overtures, were anxious to commission two new symphonies and wanted him to visit England. He asked too much money for travelling and other expenses, and was refused. By the time he was ready to reconsider, his health was too bad, and Ludwig van Beethoven never set foot in England, a country he held in much esteem and where his music had long been known.

As a result of his preoccupation with Karl and the consequent strife, his output, and thereby his income, was severely curtailed, with the further result that his fears of not being able to provide for the boy increased. Meanwhile, Johanna was being informed by Beethoven's servants on details of her son's upbringing in the Bohemian apartment of his bachelor uncle. Karl was sent to yet another boarding school at Mödling, run by Father Fröhlich, but after only one month there he was expelled for misconduct. The effects of his grotesque background were already beginning to show themselves, and would continue to do so for the rest of Beethoven's life. Yet though he was irritable and impatient with the boy's minor faults, he was indulgent over his greater misdemeanours.

In 1818 Johanna made yet another attempt through the courts to recover her son. Possibly through the influence of Beethoven's aristocratic patrons, and by misusing the 'van' in his name to make it the 'von' which denoted minor nobility in Austria (a deception he practised whenever it suited him and which it is said helped ease his way into

Viennese society), the case was given the privilege of a hearing in the Landrecht court, where the proceedings were quicker and more discreet than in ordinary courts.

Beethoven had to answer on two counts. He replied to the first by letter, but when, in the course of the action, Karl ran away from his uncle to his mother, and was brought back by the police whom Beethoven immediately called, Beethoven was ordered to appear in court in person with Karl. In giving evidence he happened to remark that if Karl had been eligible for the Theresianum he would have been sent there, thus revealing the minor deception about his name and status, and it was noticed. There is a story that when challenged to give proof of his nobility Beethoven pointed to his head and his heart and said, 'There is the proof!' This is not recorded in the transcripts, but certainly his inability to supply more tangible proof led to the case being passed down to the commoners' court, where some of the formal niceties were dispensed with.

In this court Beethoven found himself up against evidence from servants and even from Fr Fröhlich, testifying that Beethoven encouraged his nephew to speak disrespectfully of his mother and rewarded any signs of hatred the boy might show or pretend. In the end the court decided that Karl had been tossed backward and forward enough and that he had been sent to too many schools which had proved unsuitable in one way or another. It awarded Johanna custody, under nominal supervision by the State Procurator.

Beethoven had suffered a temporary setback, but with his usual tenacity he took legal advice and appealed. The evidence of Fr Fröhlich was invalid, he claimed, because he was 'a drunkard and a libertine', and he went so far as to suggest that the priest had been influenced by the sexual wiles of Johanna. Perhaps more impressively he offered as joint legal guardian his friend Karl Peters, Prince Lobkowitz's children's tutor and a man of impeccable character. On 8 April 1820 Beethoven heard that he was to be from then on Karl's sole guardian.

At last he could return to his composing. Karl was to be a source of worry and trial for the rest of his life, but it is fairly certain that the note of sudden joy which passes through the piano sonatas of this time springs from Beethoven's relief and happiness at the settlement of this case.

Sublime Achievements

1819 – 1826

THE PROTRACTED LEGAL TUSSLE which absorbed so much of Beethoven's time had never wholly stemmed the progress of his work, which included the exquisite song-cycle *An die Ferne Geliebte* ('To the Distant Lover') and the staggeringly conceived Piano Sonatas Ops.101 and 106. In 1819 he started work on a solemn Mass intended to celebrate the enthronement of his patron, Archduke Rudolph, as Archbishop of Olmütz. Underestimating both the time needed for such a task and the extent to which it would stretch his imagination, he was nowhere near ready with the work when the enthronement took place at Cologne Cathedral in March 1820.

There is little doubt that Beethoven had intended to write a setting of the Latin Mass for many years, but other claims on his time had prevented him from doing so. As soon as he heard of the Archduke's elevation his thoughts became focused, and he determined that the moment had come. He had been making a study of earlier church music and exploring the works of J.S. Bach and Handel. The latter, he asserted, was the greatest of all composers; he found the church music of Haydn and Mozart, though impressive, too light and Italianate for his taste. Even Karl was dispatched to do research on the earliest church music masters in the public museums and private libraries of Vienna. Once he had undertaken the task Beethoven found the Mass becoming a statement of his own profound, though unorthodox faith. Because it was intended for an elaborate church celebration of great splendour the scale of the work had to be appropriately magnificent, which accorded well with the cast of his mind at the time. But the larger the scale and the more inspired the work, the longer he would be engaged on it.

In the event it took five years to create the *Missa Solemnis* and Beethoven was never to see a complete performance. Sections were performed for the Archbishop, as he now was, and parts were given in Vienna, but the first full performance took place on 7 May 1824 in St Petersburg for the same Tsar of Russia who had heard his works at the Congress of Vienna ten years before. The publication of the Mass brought its problems too. Aware that it was a great work, one of the most monumental pieces of the great 'Third Period' from which sprang his deepest and most inspired compositions, Beethoven was unwilling to let it go cheaply. He put out feelers in Paris and London, but publishers, aware of the enormous difficulties involved in mounting a performance, were reluctant to take it. Though his European reputation was toweringly higher than any of his contemporaries', the work called for a full scale orchestra of talented players, a large chorus capable of mastering the extremely taxing choral writing, and four soloists of total brilliance to sing the almost impossibly difficult parts, added to which it would require almost two hours to perform. Eventually it was taken for only 600 florins by the publishing firm of Schott & Son of Mainz.

What made the *Missa Solemnis* such a lengthy undertaking was not a lack of knowledge of the various ways of setting the Latin Mass. Beethoven had already made at least two earlier versions of the Mass, the 1807 one in C major (Op.86) being a full and long setting. The *Missa Solemnis* was so different because it was written at a time when he was reappraising all his previous ideas and techniques, and in it he incorporated all the fruits of his studies of early church music. Those of his friends who saw him at the time record the great feelings of spiritual struggle that exuded from him as he worked to create music that would do justice to the meaning of the text. Over the Kyrie Eleison section he wrote the words 'Let it flow from my heart to the hearts of all men', revealing how seriously he regarded his purpose in the undertaking. Like *Fidelio*, in which he also saw a moral duty as well as a musical challenge, the work cannot be described in words and it must be heard to appreciate its gigantic scope and magnitude: the Kyrie, so totally conveying the meaning of 'Lord have mercy upon us'; the elevation of spirit which attends the Gloria; the assertion of total faith and power in the breathtaking Credo; the Benedictus, with its soaring violin solos and hushed choral voices; the prayer and awe of Dona Nobis Pacem; and the transcendent finale of the Agnus Dei which brings the work to a triumphant end.

Beethoven thought of the *Missa Solemnis* as his greatest work. Most musicians would not agree with this judgement. Certainly, it had cost him immense labours and massive internal struggle, and the final product of these, unimaginable from any other composer, may be the greatest Mass ever written. But it was two years later, in 1824, that there emerged what might with more complete justice be claimed his greatest work: the Ninth Symphony.

Approaching his mid-fifties, with his health inexorably deteriorating and his hearing gone, Beethoven worked at fever pitch. After the huge-scale effort of the *Missa Solemnis* he had turned to the more intimate form of the dazzling and fecund *Diabelli Variations* for piano, and to the first of that last series of string quartets which, in their different way, embody his musical genius at its height. Although his friends knew that he was more active in composition in his deafness and isolation than he had ever been in the days when public performance was still possible for him, the Viennese public believed that the grand old man of music in their city had written himself out. The music of Rossini and other Italians was in vogue, but not entirely to everyone's satisfaction, so when word escaped that Beethoven was working on a new symphony the excitement among the music-loving public was immense.

In fact, Beethoven intended the work for the Philharmonic Society of London, and wrote to his former pupil Ferdinand Ries, living in England and acting as intermediary, to find out how much they would pay for the rights to the finished work for eighteen months. It is an indication of his financial state that he was prepared to accept the £50 which they offered him. 'I would write gratis for those leading artists of Europe if I were not poor Beethoven,' he wrote to Ries.

The *Missa Solemnis* had been Beethoven's great spiritual testament, and the Ninth Symphony was to be his great assertion of human worth. On a similar scale to the Mass, it requires orchestral playing of the highest calibre, and - an astonishing innovation at the time - has a choral finale, which was thought unsingably difficult. Vast in conception and magnificently unpredictable though the first three movements are, it was this finale, the first choral fourth movement of a symphony ever, which took its first hearers by storm. Beethoven had chosen a poem he had long admired and had toyed with for appropriate musical setting off and on for almost as long as he had lived in Vienna, Schiller's *An die Freude* ('Ode to Joy'). A hymn in praise of human brotherhood and universal friendship, it was completely in tune with Beethoven's personal philosophy of life, and it drew from him such variety of treatment and breadth of imaginative vision that it was recognised from its first performance as the very pinnacle of his achievement.

That first performance was given on 7 May 1824 - in Vienna. Although the symphony was the exclusive property of the Philharmonic Society of London, Beethoven was determined that his personal public should be the first to hear it. The concert would be given in the Kärntnertortheater and would also include parts of the *Missa Solemnis*.

The rehearsals were not an easy affair. There were only two of them, and the work required a huge force of players and singers. The latter constantly complained that their parts were impossible. Beethoven ignored them; he knew what could and what could not be sung, though even he would have admitted that it was not easy, and could not have heard the result anyway. By the 7th, however, everything had been finalised. Only one matter remained; who would conduct? By now even Beethoven realised that for him to undertake this task unaided was ludicrous, so Ignaz Umlauf, who had been responsible for conducting *Fidelo's* successful 1822 revival, was called upon to direct the orchestra, with Beethoven standing beside him to indicate tempi throughout.

The crowded concert must remain one of the most memorable of all time. Such was the effect of the earlier movements of the Ninth that they were applauded individually. Finally came that electrifying unity of orchestra, soloists and huge chorus, building up to a controlled frenzy of praise and joy such as had never before been heard:

> *Freude schöner Götterfunken,*
> *Tochter aus Elysium...*

When it was over, the hall erupted. In Vienna it was the custom that the royal family were applauded four times whenever they made a public appearance. To the consternation of officials and police, Beethoven was applauded *five* times.

Among the many poignant anecdotes surrounding the deaf Beethoven, none can be sadder than the account of the end of this, his most triumphant concert. As the applause roared and swelled throughout the hall singers and conductor took their bows. No one thought of Beethoven until the young contralto soloist Caroline Unger noticed him still standing with head bowed, his back to the audience whose cheers he could not hear. It was not until she turned him round that he realized what he had achieved.

Beethoven's attitude to his nephew and ward Karl continued to be intensely over-protective. The entries in the conversation notebooks show how, from the best-intentioned motives, he continually cross-questioned him about his activities, habits and way of life. He seems to have overlooked that in the ten years since his father's death the boy had grown into a man with friends of his own and a natural need for independence. In the light of Beethoven's own uncertain way of life and irregular income he was anxious to see Karl securely settled in a safe career. Karl, however, was intent on joining the army. Beethoven, who had twice seen the invasion and occupation of his adopted home city, and heard his *Fidelio* jeered at by soldiers, found the idea anathema. He was still financing Karl's existence, and felt entitled to decide what was best for the boy. Consequently, in 1825, Karl was entered to read philosophy at the university in Vienna. His time there was short. Sure that he would fail examinations because he found the subject so dull, he persuaded his uncle to remove him and let him study at the polytechnic institute for a business career. Beethoven was not too upset at this move, which seemed at least to foreshadow a safe career for Karl.

Though Beethoven behaved in seemingly unworthy ways towards Karl, his actions were all prompted by the inordinate love he felt for the boy whom he always addressed in letters as 'son'. He spied on his activities, getting friends to accompany him into taverns to see if he was a heavy drinker and watch whether he gambled much at billiards. He was also concerned for Karl's sexual welfare. Whether or not Beethoven did suffer at some time from venereal disease, he had certainly been with prostitutes and knew of the potential dangers. When one of his brothers first came to Vienna he had written him a letter advising him to 'beware of decaying fortresses; assaulting them is more costly than assaulting well-kept ones', and he was determined to preserve Karl from such risks. He asked his friend Karl Holz, closer in years to Karl, to steer him away from the city's red-light areas. In an attempt to 'improve' Karl's cultural tastes he offered him sums of money if he would attend some 'improving' piece in the Burgtheater twice a week. Not surprisingly, Karl's attitude was to take the very opposite course to that his uncle wished. Beethoven's letters to Karl reveal a lonely and pathetic man struggling against ill-health and worrying excessively over a boy who was now almost a man.

But there must have been some justification in

Karl's rebellious attitude, to judge from some of the one-sided accounts of the conversation books...

> You think it is insolence when, after reproaching me undeservedly for hours... I cannot pass instantly from bitter feelings of pain to pleasantry. I am not so lighthearted as you think...
> ... After all, I am 20!

When Beethoven discovered that Karl had been 'borrowing' small sums of money from the house-keeping funds to buy the things which he, considering them unnecessary, would not pay for, he flew into a tirade of self-pity and reproach:

> God is my witness, I dream only of getting away from you and from this wretched brother and that horrible family which has been thrust on me. God grant my wishes, for I can no longer trust you.
> Unfortunately your father
> or, better still, not your father!

During 1826 Karl also began seeing his mother again. Beethoven furiously offered him the alternatives of going back permanently to her or staying with him and seeing no more of her. His uncle interfered in every aspect of the boy's life, even down to ordering his clothes for him and saw no reason for Karl to need cash of his own. But Karl did need cash, and as his exams approached he foresaw certain failure and an unpleasant scene with his creditors. Consequently, at Baden on 30 July, he went off to the Rauhenstein castle ruins and put a pistol to his head. If it was an attempt on his life it was a failure, either because it was not seriously meant or because he was, in the words of Beethoven's biographer, Thayer, 'a bungler with firearms'. He was found by some people attracted by the noise and taken to his mother's lodgings nearby.

Beethoven was informed, as the boy's legal guardian, and asked his friend Holz to go immediately and look into the affair. Meanwhile the boy's mother, in sending for a doctor in haste, had caused the local police to interest themselves in the case.

Suicide was illegal and regarded as a form of lunacy, so the boy was taken into protective custody in a nearby hospital and a magistrate appointed to look into the reasons for the attempt. To make his apparent madness more likely, Karl would throw a fit every time his uncle's name was mentioned and threatened to tear his bandages off his wounded head if it were mentioned again. In the gossip of Vienna, Beethoven emerged as the monstrous tyrant uncle and Karl as the poor boy driven by cruelty and deprivation. The effect of this event and its subsequent humiliating repercussions was shattering both to Beethoven's pride and health. Friends claimed that overnight he came to look as if he were seventy - in fact he was fifty-six.

The outcome for Karl was better. After release from hospital, under Austrian law he had to enter a religious house where brothers could watch him lest he tried suicide again, and where they could also teach him the folly of his actions. It became apparent that the best thing was to allow him to enter the army, just as he had intended two unhappy years before. Beethoven bowed to the inevitable and prevailed on the von Breuning family, his old Bonn friends, to use their influence to get Karl a cadetship. He seems to have been relatively happy in the army, and Beethoven dedicated one of his late string quartets to his regimental commander, Baron von Stutterheim. Karl remained Beethoven's heir and even grew to cherish the memory of his uncle, realizing that he had acted in a misguided way but with the best of intentions.

As for Beethoven, a dramatic downturn in his already chronic ill-health soon drove Karl and his mother out of his thoughts.

Last Suffering

1826 – 1827

IN OCTOBER 1826 Beethoven took Karl with him on a late holiday to his brother Johann's estate in Gneixendorf, by the Danube. Even though Johann was not the best of hosts, eventually charging his brother for board and lodgings, Beethoven stayed there until December, working on the last String Quartets. He found a new finale for the one in B flat major, first performed earlier that year with the *Grosse Fuge* as its finale. He also wrote the greater part of the F major Quartet (Op.135), a lovely, haunted acknowledgement of death's beckoning presence.

It was noticed that his feet and stomach were badly swollen and bandaged, but he had accustomed himself and those about him to his poor health. He had only light summer clothes with him, and the journey back to Vienna by lurching cart in wintry December weather, with an overnight stay at an unheated inn, had bad effects on him. During that night he was seized with a painful cough, which he tried to assuage by drinking large quantities of iced water. By the time he reached Vienna he was in a state of collapse. A doctor diagnosed pleurisy, which soon developed into pneumonia. He had a searing pain in his side, spat blood constantly, and almost choked during frequent coughing spasms. A week later he was somewhat recovered, though, and able to hobble about his rooms; but the dropsy which had been noticed at Gneixendorf increased and he swelled up alarmingly. Acute symptoms of jaundice added to his distress.

During his last illness he hardly left his rooms at all. His friends rallied round, realizing that their great genius, whom they had bribed and supported for so long to stay in Vienna, might very soon be taken from them by powers which no money could buy off. They brought gifts of all sorts, including the collected works of Handel, whom he called 'the master of all masters', and he delighted in reading and studying them up to two days before his death. He was also visited by the young composer Franz Schubert, who had long viewed Beethoven from a reverential distance in the city. Beethoven was too ill for the visits to have any other than emotional significance for the doomed younger man, who wrote of him:

> He can do everything, but we cannot yet understand all that he does, and a lot of water will flow under the Danube bridges before this man's creations are generally understood... Mozart's relationship to Beethoven is like Schiller's to Shakespeare; Schiller is already understood, but Shakespeare by no means.

Perhaps the only joy that Beethoven had on his deathbed was in the company of Stephen von Breuning's thirteen-year-old son Gerhard. Missing Karl, even though they had quarrelled so often, Beethoven delighted in the boy's conversation and was touched by his concern. The lad ran minor errands for him, and even tried to relieve his condition. An entry appears in the conversation books: 'I believe you suffer badly from bed bugs. So that when you sleep you are woken up by them. Since sleep is necessary and good for you I will bring you something to get rid of them.' But Beethoven's state was becoming so serious that bed bugs were a minor concern.

In January 1827 he had to be operated on to drain off the fluids which had accumulated from his dropsy. Foolishly, he demanded the attentions of a doctor he had relied on in earlier days, Joseph Malfatti, who told him to discard his current medicines and take a punch which he prescribed, applying cold fomentations and have warm dry-baths. The effect was disastrous; the drink brought on diarrhoea and the vapour from the baths made him swell up again, so that he seemed in danger of bursting and had to be tapped for fluids through the previous wound which had not yet had time to heal.

'The condition of the liver is the key to the whole illness,' wrote one of the doctors in Beethoven's conversation book. He had suffered for many years from what we would now call hepatitis, and at the post-mortem examination it was found that his liver had shrunk to less than half the normal size and was covered in nodules as big as beans. The hepatitis, however, was only a symptom among many. Judging the contemporary accounts in the light of modern knowledge, it seems that his whole immunity system had been impaired for a long time prior to his final illness.

On 14 March 1827, Beethoven, who had often raged against his condition, wrote, 'I am resigned and will accept whatever fate may bring.' Forty-eight hours before he died he told his watchers to send for a priest. He received the last sacraments on the afternoon of 24 March, and that evening fell into the final coma. The thirteen-year-old Gerhard von Breuning, who was still allowed into the sordid death-chamber, gave an account of those last two days of four months' indescribable illness and torment:

> The strong man lay completely unconscious in the process of dissolution, breathing so stertorously that the rattle could be heard at a distance. His powerful frame and his unweakened lungs fought with approaching death like giants. The spectacle was fearful.

At five o'clock in the afternoon of 26 March, during a thunderstorm, Beethoven died: he was fifty-six. The only people with him just then were his detested sister-in-law Johanna, and his friend Anselm Hüttenbrenner, who recorded the dramatic passing:

Beethoven lay in the final agony, the death-rattle
in his throat, from 3 o'clock until after 5 o'clock;
then there was suddenly a loud clap of thunder
accompanied by a bolt of lightning which illumin-
ated the death-chamber... Beethoven opened his
eyes, raised his right hand, and looked upwards
for several seconds with his fist clenched and with
a threatening expression which seemed to say, 'I
defy you, powers of evil! God is with me!...' As he
let his hand sink on to the bed again his eyes half
closed. My right hand lay under his head, my left
resting on his breast. Not another breath, not a
heartbeat more!

Three days after his death Beethoven's funeral
service was conducted in the local parish church in
the Alserstrasse. More than 20,000 people thronged
the neighbourhood, so that it took more than an
hour and a half for the cortège to wend its way little
more than half a mile from the house in the
Schwarzspanierstrasse. Every musician and artist of
note was there, with the entire aristocracy and some
of the Court. Schubert was a torchbearer, as was
Beethoven's pupil and friend, Czerny. Eight musicians carried the coffin, among them Hummel and
the dedicatee of the great violin sonata Op.47,
Rodolphe Kreutzer.

At the graveside at the Währing cemetery two of
Beethoven's trombone *Equali* were played and impressively sung to Latin texts. The funeral march
from the Op.26 Piano Sonata was played by a band,
and a funeral oration, written by Vienna's leading
poet, Franz Grillparzer, was spoken by Anschütz,
the principal actor from the Burgtheater. It cont-
ained the lines,'He was an artist... Who comes after
him will not follow the same path; he will have to
start anew, for he who went first did not stop until he
had reached the place where all art stops.'

Over the grave a pyramid in stone was erected with
the one word BEETHOVEN on it. His remains lay
there for sixty years, until in 1888 they were reinterred
in the newly created Grove of Honour in the vast
Central Cemetery, in a grave next to Schubert, who
had died just over a year after Beethoven.

Beethoven's sole heir was his nephew Karl, who was too far away with his regiment to attend the funeral. He inherited a trifling amount of cash and savings, and his uncle's possessions, which were sold off at public auction. The manuscripts and autographed scores all came under the hammer, for ridiculously small sums: '4th Symphony - 6 florins; Gloria from *Missa Solemnis* - 3 florins; 5th Symphony - 6 Florins; andante from *Pastoral* Symphony - 2 florins...'

When they had watched his burial on that spring day in 1827, his colleagues and friends were no longer in any doubt that the grave was claiming the greatest composer of their age, possibly of any. His list of works to which he had seen fit to give an opus number totalled a staggering 135 major creations, most of them on the large scale. It included nine symphonies, five piano concertos, a violin concerto, a triple concerto, many other works for orchestra and solo instrument, overtures, much theatre music, including a great opera, *Fidelio*, two full-scale settings of the Mass, oratorios and church music, chamber music of all kinds and for all combinations of instruments, songs and song-cycles, and a huge output for solo instruments, notably the piano, for which he had left the greatest collection of sonatas, variations and other pieces ever written by one composer. The list is staggering, especially considering how painstaking his methods of composition were, and how disordered and fraught his life. What no listing can convey is the quality and effect of those works, individually and cumulatively. Fortunately, all have been recorded - a complete collection was issued in 1970 to mark the 200th anniversary of his birth - so they are available for all to marvel at and enjoy.

Beethoven was not an innovator of musical form. The symphony he found ready-made by Haydn, who had transformed it from a one-movement 'overture' into a major work of four contrasting movements. What makes the nine symphonies the greatest collection ever produced is the quality of inventiveness with which Beethoven's constantly fruitful imagination invested the existing form. The same is true to a lesser extent of the piano concertos: the earlier ones could have been written by Mozart in robust vein, and only the *Emperor* shows the expansive and virtuoso qualities which point the way to the vast showpieces of the Romantic era.

Perhaps none of his works attain such heights, or reveal greater depths of spiritual turmoil, than the string quartets and piano sonatas. In the last of these he explored harmonic and melodic possibilities in ways that no other composer was even to consider emulating until almost a century after his death. His chromatic experiments provided the harmonic outline for Wagner and Richard Strauss, with their rich and harmonically imaginative scoring. It is more true of Beethoven than of any other that no subsequent composer has been uninfluenced by him: his output forms the keystone on which the whole Romantic movement is founded. Without his example the products of Brahms, Liszt, Wagner, Mahler and many others is unimaginable.

Beethoven was also the first composer to be self-supporting. Although his successors would continue to teach for money and accept financial backing, it would be on the basis of his pioneering example of proud independence and freedom from interference.

The more one studies and listens to Beethoven's music the more appropriate that comparison with Shakespeare seems. As Shakespeare touched on virtually every feeling and emotion, and left a comment of penetrating insight on it, so Beethoven used every musical form to express the power and greatness of the human spirit and imagination. The paradox of what many consider to be the greatest of all music having come from a deaf man is obvious, but Beethoven's life exemplifies something else: that the human spirit is capable of rising above illness, poverty, circumstances in which creation would seem impossible to attempt, to produce such profound, beautiful and uplifting artistic achievement.

Beethoven

1770 – 1827

Lodewijk van Beethoven (1712-1773). The composer's
grandfather.

Johann and Maria Magdalena van Beethoven, the
composer's parents.

Bonn, Beethoven's birthplace. A contemporary engraving showing an elegant and tranquil town on the banks of the unspoilt Rhine.

Formerly 515 Bongasse, now the Beethovenhaus Museum. The family occupied only the back attic flat where the composer was born in December 1770.

Advertisement for Beethoven's first public performance, falsely claiming the player to be only six years old.

Maximilian Friedrich (1708-1784), Elector and Archbishop of Cologne.

Maximilian Franz (1756-1801), Archduke of Austria, Archbishop and Elector of Cologne from 1784.

Christian Gottlob Neefe (1748-1798). Appointed court organist in 1781 he recognised Beethoven's genius and guided him through the theory of music and also awakened in him a love of the classical authors in literature and philosophy.

Beethoven c. 1784 at the age of 13. The earliest known portrait.

The Breuning family house in Bonn. Beethoven gave music lessons to Eleonore, daughter of this cultivated, upper-middle class family with whom he spent so many happy days in his youth.

The market place in Bonn, with its fountain and Town Hall in the background. A busy and popular meeting place. One of Beethoven's favourite eating houses, the Zehrgarten, is on the right.

A delightful family silhouette of the Breuning family. Eleonore stands listening as her mother reads.

A view of Vienna in the late 18th century.

The young composer.

The young Beethoven playing before Mozart. Mozart said to a companion, 'Keep your eyes on him; some day he will give the world something to talk about.'

Bonn at the end of the 18th century.
In November 1792 the composer
left for his second journey to
Vienna, never to return to his
birthplace.

Joseph Haydn (1732-1809). The senior
musical figure of his day. While eventually
Beethoven moved away from the general direction
of Haydn's traditional approach, he always had
the greatest respect and his first six String Quartets
Op.18 were dedicated to Haydn.

Antonio Salieri (1750-
1825). Imperial Court
Kapellmeister from
1788. He was Mozart's
bitter rival but much
admired as a teacher by
his many pupils,
including Beethoven.

The famous silhouette of the young Beethoven.

Beethoven conducts a Rasumowsky Quartet at a concert typical of those held in the private palaces of the musically dedicated nobility.

Vienna, a contemporary engraving of a view of the Graben towards the Kohlmarkt. Beethoven once lived in this street at 214 Graben. In his 35 years in Vienna, ever restless, he moved some thirty times.

Beethoven's viola from his time in Bonn.

Copy of the score of the String Trio in E flat major Op.3.

The Royal Palace of King Frederick William II of Prussia, in Berlin, where during a visit in 1796 Beethoven played several times at the Court of the appreciative monarch.

The Kohlmarkt in Vienna. Beethoven's publishers, Artaria & Co., can be seen in the right foreground.

King Frederick William II, devoted to music and famed as having one of the finest orchestras in Europe. He gave Beethoven a gold snuff box full of gold coins, a gift of which he was exceedingly proud.

Prince Karl Lichnowsky (1756-1814), an early patron of Beethoven in Vienna.

Grande Sonate pathétique
Pour le Clavecin ou Piano Forte
Composée et Dédiée
A Son Altesse Monseigneur le Prince
CHARLES DE LICHNOWSKY
par
Louis Van Beethoven
Oeuvre 13.
Beÿ Joseph Eder am Graben.

Title-page of the *Pathétique* Sonata, Op.13, dedicated to Prince Lichnowsky.

Beethoven's quartet instruments, two violins, a viola and a cello, gifts from Prince Karl Lichnowsky.

Vienna, Stock am Eisen Platz, an engraving from 1779.

Beethoven in 1802.
A miniature
painted on ivory by
Christian Hornemann.

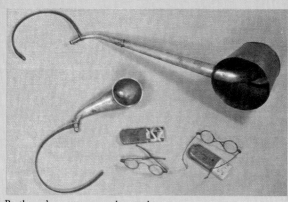

Beethoven's ear trumpets and spectacles.

Contemporary view of Heiligenstadt where in 1802 he came to terms with his increasing deafness.

The 'Heiligenstadt Testament' dated 6 October 1802.

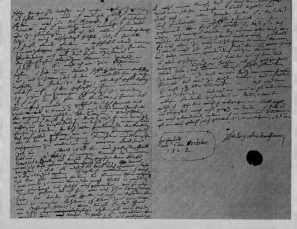

Beethoven in 1804, aged 34.
A highly stylised, romantic
portrait

Countess Giulietta Guicciardi (1784-1856),
a pupil. Beethoven became deeply attached
to her and dedicated the *Moonlight* Sonata to
her.

Prince Franz Joseph von Lobkowitz (1772-1816). A noble benefactor.

Title page of the original edition of the *Eroica* Symphony.

Corrected title page to the manuscript score of the *Eroica* Symphony. So heavily had Beethoven scratched out Napoleon's name that he tore a hole in the paper.

Theater-an-der-Wien. This theatre saw the first public performance of the *Eroica* Symphony, 7 April 1805, and a number of other major works by Beethoven.

Countess Therese von Brunswick (1775-1861). One of Beethoven's many loves. He kept a copy of this portrait she gave him until his death.

One of the famous 'Immortal Beloved' letters.

The house in Döbling where the composer worked on the *Eroica* Symphony.

Beethoven, a contemporary engraving.

Theatre bill for the first performance of *Fidelio*, 20 November 1805.

Scene from *Fidelio*, Beethoven's only opera.

Scène from *Fidelio*.

Title page from the manuscript score of *Fidelio*.

Theatre bill for the later, revised version of *Fidelio*, 23 May 1814.

One of Beethoven's many pianos. This one was
bought for him by Prince Lichnowsky.

A later romantic interpretation of Beethoven
composing the *Pastoral* Symphony.

Prince Ferdinand Kinsky (1782-1812). A wealthy patron.

Archduke Rudolph of Austria (1788-1831). Together with Prince Lobkowitz and Prince Kinsky an agreement dated 1 March 1809 was made to provide a pension for Beethoven to prevent his leaving Vienna for the Court of King Jerome.

Title page for the *Pastoral* Symphony, first performed in public on 22 December 1808.

Johann van Beethoven (1776- 1848), the composer's younger brother.

Johann Wolfgang von Goethe (1749-1832). Beethoven's first meeting with Goethe was in July 1812.

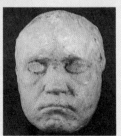

Life mask by F. Klein.
Taken in 1812 this is the most
factual representation of
Beethoven.

Plaster bust by Klein,
working from the life mask.

A Beethoven Sonata. A painting by L. Balestrieri.
(Note the life mask on the wall).

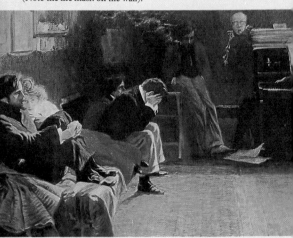

Beethoven in 1818.

Marble bust of the composer.

Beethoven in 1815.

An engraving of 1820.

Bronze bust.

Friends listening to Beethoven playing
one of his compositions.

Inset - Karl,
Beethoven's nephew.

Imperial Court Theatre where the first public
performance of the Ninth Symphony took place on 7
May 1824.

Title page of the *Missa
Solemnis*.

Title page of the Ninth
Symphony.

A contemporary view of Baden, where Beethoven
often went for treatment and for rest.

Beethoven in 1823.

Beethoven's workroom sketched just before his death.

The composer just before his death on 26 March 1827.

Beethoven's ha
sketched at his
holding a cross

Beethoven on his death bed.

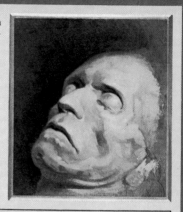

Beethoven's funeral. More than 20,000 people attended.

Inset - Franz Grillparzer (1791-1872), Vienna's leading poet and Beethoven's friend who wrote the funeral oration.

Beethoven's death mask.

The composer's grave in the Central Cemetery in Vienna.

ACKNOWLEDGEMENTS

The author and publishers would like to thank the following for their kind
permission in supplying the illustrations in this book.

Archiv für Kunst und Geschichte, Berlin
Beethoven Archiv, Bonn
Beethoven-Haus, Bonn
H.C. Bodmer Collection, Beethoven-Haus, Bonn
British Library, London
Graphische Sammlung Albertina, Vienna
Historisches Museum der Stadt, Vienna
Bildarchiv der Österreichische Nationalbibliothek, Vienna
Schloss Hradec, Czechoslovakia
Collection Senator Otto Reichert, Vienna
Stadtarchiv und Wissenschaftliche Stadtbibliothek, Bonn
Evergreen Lives Archive